CAITLIN,

THANKS FOR THE
MANY WAYS YOU
HELP MAKE D.A.
SUCH A SPECIAL
PLACE!

Jeff

THE GREAT TEAM TURNA ROUND

How to unlock growth using PVTV™
and The Great Game of Business™

JEFF HILIMIRE

"This is the formula for how every team should run!"
- Jack Stack

First printing 2021

Book design by Michael Stanley and Najdan Mancic

ISBN 978-1-7338689-5-2

Published by Ripples Media

www.ripples.media

"The future is not a gift. It is an achievement."

—*Bobby Kennedy*

DEDICATION

While I've had the chance to be part of some incredible teams, my favorite by far is our team at home (affectionately called the 7Mires). Emily, Zac, Drew, Kaitlyn, Hannah, and Kai, I love you all so much.

Since this is a book about teams, I would be remiss if I didn't also dedicate this book to my favorite tennis teammates: Danny Davis, Tony Duda, Jeff Kuchma (Rocketman!), and Sasha Parc. You guys are the greatest.

And to our coach, Jim Boykin, who I hold in the highest regard. Thank you for showing me what it meant to be a leader at such a young age. Your influence on me and my teammates is immeasurable.

CONTENTS

FOREWORD

Everything Begins with Inspiration

All of us could use more inspiration in our lives. Someone once defined inspiration to me as when we receive and communicate sacred revelations. That sounds pretty heavy, but also true. If I were to try and define inspiration in my own words, I might equate it with that feeling of gratitude we sometimes get in our hearts when we're moved to tears or to take action.

By writing *The Great Team Turnaround*, Jeff Hilimire is trying to inspire people to take action. He wants the readers of this book to recognize that there is a better way for us to work together on a daily basis than the outdated rules passed down from the Industrial Society; he wants readers to embrace the idea that work doesn't have to be unsatisfying and that when you teach people the rules of business, how to keep score, and how to earn a stake in the outcome, they might actually start to have some fun on the job—and find the inspiration to achieve just like Jeff used to do on the tennis court back in his college days.

I find it both flattering and embarrassing that Jeff features me as a character in the pages that follow. He credits me for inspiring him to embrace the leadership system that many of us created together nearly forty years ago called, "The Great Game of Business."

But the story doesn't start with me. I, too, was inspired by so many others on my own personal journey to rethink how we work—and maybe have some fun doing it.

My career started decades ago in the mailroom of a Fortune 500 manufacturing company that employed more than one hundred thousand people. I was an observer and a people watcher. My job gave me the opportunity to listen to the angst and disgust, as well as the wishes and hopes, of people throughout every level of the organization.

I heard how people made fun of supervisors behind their backs, mocking them for their stiff ties and clipboards as they barked orders. The supervisors didn't understand that all anyone wanted was to be given the freedom to think and to make a difference. Meanwhile, the supervisors would pull their hair out wondering why the folks on the frontline were so disengaged and unproductive. They were two teams chasing the same goal but working against each other instead.

In time, as I rose through the ranks, I became a suit. But I didn't want to be that guy everyone laughed at. So I began to share sacred revelations—information and facts with the frontline folks. I knew they knew how to do the job better than anyone else. But they were often doing it with incomplete information. No one explained the big picture to them. To them, they were just asked to do their job, nothing more, nothing less.

The change in our team was immediate and remarkable. Frowns turned into smiles. People began to understand that it wasn't enough to just meet their own individual goals. They would win only if they were inspired to play together. And their self-confidence soared as a result.

I ran this same experiment again and again over the next decade as I took on different assignments inside the company. I taught departments to understand how they relied on one another. I wanted to show them that it wasn't good enough to hit goals and set records if you didn't understand how your performance impacted the departments connected upstream and downstream.

You could be knocking it out of the park on a production side until the day you run out of parts. Then you start screaming at the parts guys, blaming them for slowing you down, only to realize you had never told them what your goals were. Or why the sales team was yelling at production because their customers were getting angry waiting for a delivery, only to realize that they hadn't talked to the delivery team about what they were pushing out the door.

By getting people to stop working in silos—and competing against one another—they began to realize that we all should be focused on the same goal: building an outrageously successful company, together.

That idea is at the very root of The Great Game of Business. When we give people the information and the education to do their jobs, create a scoreboard for them to shoot for shared goals, and then share the rewards with them when they're successful, anything is possible—including turnarounds.

In 1986, *Inc.* magazine ran an article with the headline "The Turnaround" about a fledgling company called Springfield Remanufacturing Company—now called SRC—that my associates and I spun out from our struggling corporate parent. We did it out of necessity—they were going to close our plant otherwise. We wanted to save our jobs. We doubled down on the lessons we had learned up to that point and made the decision to run the entire business using those same principles of transparency, openness, and collaboration. It was the best decision we could have ever made.

By working together, our now 1,800 associates have not only built an outrageously successful company, but they also share in that success as 100% employee owners of the business.

In 1993, this idea we had been working on became a book titled *The Great Game of Business*. What we didn't count on was how many people like Jeff Hilimire would read that book years later and somehow find inspiration inside of it.

We're incredibly humbled that thousands of companies of all sizes and in every industry—from small businesses around the world to household names like Netflix, Southwest Airlines, and Chick-fil-A—have also been inspired to rethink how they can get their team engaged at work like never before by playing The Great Game.

I believe that in the pages of Jeff's book, he paints a picture of a better way to run a business—one that combines the power of his PVTV model with the principals of The Great Game. I applaud him for making the connection between the need for teams to shoot for a higher purpose and to embrace values with the need for an operational system like The Great Game to make it happen on a daily basis. Otherwise, you'll just end up with a scrap of yellowing parchment hanging on your wall.

My hope is that after reading Jeff's story you, too, will be inspired to take action. When that happens, we can change the world. God bless.

Jack Stack

President and CEO of SRC Holdings Corporation and
author of The Great Game of Business.

PRELUDE

This book is the third installment of *The Turnaround Leadership Series* and begins immediately after completing *The 5-Day Turnaround*. As with the previous two books, this one is a fictional narrative. Many of the characters you will meet, including the protagonist, Will, exist in the first two books.

The Great Team Turnaround is an essential element of the series. It more fully brings to life Purpose, Vision, Tenets & Values (PVTV) and introduces a new, pivotal concept to the reader, The Great Game of Business (GGOB).

When you start an endeavor like a book, you never know what will resonate most with the audience. The reception of my PVTV concept in the first two books was overwhelmingly positive. Many people have asked for more information to help them implement the process in their business. I was excited to see PVTV rise to the top because I know it is the most critical aspect of the concepts I have introduced.

And thus, this book dives deeper into each of these pillars. You'll learn more about Purpose, Vision, Tenets & Values and how to create and unleash PVTV within your team.

This book also shows the potential of unlocking the power of the GGOB by connecting it to a company's PVTV. I have long been a follower of The Great Game, devouring Jack Stack's books along the way. While powerful and uniting, PVTV lacked a fundamental aspect until I learned more about GGOB. In this book, I will show the power of the GGOB while providing clarity on the process of bringing your PVTV to life.

I think what you'll find is the same thing I learned as I have used this combination to build my businesses. The organization or team that runs both PVTV and GGOB is nothing short of unstoppable.

As the book opens, we find Will at the conference where our story last ended. He is preparing to give the opening keynote, speaking on building an entrepreneurial, growing business through the use of PVTV. He published his book, *The 5-Day Turnaround*, three months prior and has spent more and more time consulting, finding his true passion in helping leaders build great teams.

I hope you enjoy being on this journey with me,

Jeff

THE GREAT TEAM
TURNAROUND

If all else fails, picture everyone naked.

That's the advice that Rachel gave me as I stepped up to deliver my keynote speech. Although I'd be speaking to the largest crowd I'd ever been in front of—some 1,500 people—I didn't feel very nervous. I must not have been giving off a vibe of confidence, though, because Rachel added, "And remember, Eric and I are out here, so we'll be sure to laugh at all your corny jokes."

As I started to make my way to the stage, she grabbed my arm and added, "But . . . how about not picturing *us* naked."

Indeed.

Rachel is the newly appointed president of my advertising agency. She had been my head of operations for many years and was our most loyal and dedicated team member. It was an easy decision to promote her to this new leadership role. She was ready, probably a lot sooner than I realized.

Eric is the chief growth officer of our largest client, Titan. Eighteen months earlier, I had helped Titan's marketing team evolve to be more agile, trusting, and entrepreneurial. At the time, Matt was the chief marketing officer. Because of his team's successful transformation, Matt moved up into the role of chief growth officer, a position we had created during the process to encompass more of his new responsibilities. I had also put the experience to use, writing a book called *The 5-Day Turnaround*, loosely based on our work.

The book had done so well that other companies and teams had requested help acting more like successful startups. That led me to do more speaking and consulting. In the months following that book release, my time had gone into this new consulting practice. And that led me to realize it was time for Rachel to take over the agency side of the business.

As I weaved through the tables on my way to the stage, Eric caught my eye. Giving him a friendly fist bump as I passed, I was struck by how different our relationship was now from when we first met. He had been a difficult participant at the start of *The 5-Day Turnaround* work, yet he had taken a 180-degree turn by the time we finished. He was now the biggest proponent of the process, even going so far as to give me advice along the way, helping me continue evolving the model.

I was going to spend the next 45 minutes (plus 15 minutes of Q&A) speaking to attendees who were hoping to learn about "Evolving Leadership." My focus within this conference theme was the topic that had become the most helpful section of my book: Purpose, Vision, Tenets & Values (PVTV).

PVTV was a core component of our agency, and it had become the most critical component of Titan's success over the last year and a half. I'd seen its impact firsthand. PVTV could give any organization or team their best chance of being as effective and as inspired as possible.

My opening slide was broadcast on massive monitors to either side of where I'd speak. It read, "Realize Your Full Potential Through PVTV." It wasn't the catchiest of titles, but I had opted for directness over something pithy.

Actually, this wasn't my opening slide. It was my only slide.

I always preferred to speak free of slides or notes, relying on my preparation. It gave me the ability to react to the mood of the audience. My process was to memorize the opening five minutes, so if I was nervous (and picturing everyone naked didn't help), I could find my momentum through the memorized bits. Then I would have a mental model of the talk, literally envisioning the speech and the key points or personal stories that would trigger a move to the next section.

During preparation, I'd spend hours practicing the speech (usually while driving), asking Siri for reminders if something occurred to me as I went through the paces. Luckily, we've all become so used to connecting to the phone in our cars via Bluetooth that it probably didn't look too odd as I passed other commuters, talking and laughing to no one.

Stepping up to the mic, I started as I always do, with a joke. The tried-and-true method lightened the mood. It also let the audience know the talk would be casual and engaging and that it would be okay to laugh at my (sometimes corny) jokes.

"I'm so honored to be here today," I said. "But, if I'm honest, being here was a bit of luck. See, Julie and her team always put on such a great event. When she thought about who would be great as the keynote speaker, she asked the best public speaker she knew. Unfortunately for her, that person politely declined. So then she asked the most intelligent person she knew, and sadly, once again, that person had to decline. She was starting to worry but still had the most accomplished person she knew to ask. That person turned her down too!"

Light laughter filled the room. I went on.

"So when she called to ask if I'd do it, I said, 'Julie, this is the fourth time you've asked me. Okay, fine! You got me. I'll deliver the keynote.'"

The joke lit up the room. I was off and running. From that point, the talk went well.

When I finished my part of the speech, we opened the floor for Q&A. People lined up at the microphones set up around the room to ask questions. I'd fielded a few softballs when a young man stepped up to the mic and asked, "This all sounds great, and I have a ton of notes about PVTV that I hope to implement at my company after the conference. But my question for you is, where is the accountability in this model? I read in your book, *The 5-Day Turnaround*, that your mentor said that 'what gets measured gets done,' but I don't see a measurement model attached to PVTV."

Huh.

Nobody had ever asked that question. He was right. While PVTV was a model for creating a foundation of belief and understanding within a team, I had never put a measurement mechanism in place. At my company and the few businesses I'd consulted, we based the success of PVTV on a sense of how well it was going. This loose measurement was, admittedly, a massive oversight on my part. After all, an entire section of the five core principles that make up *The 5-Day Turnaround* is about the importance of measurement.

Usually quick on my feet, I stammered a bit.

"That's a good question," I said, deciding to be honest. "Currently, there isn't a specific model for measuring the impact and progress of a team's Purpose, Vision, Tenets & Values. I suppose each team or company I've seen implement PVTV has found their own ways of measuring it, admittedly often by gut feeling. I think you've hit on something important that I'll need to spend time on."

We moved on to the next person, but my mind stayed on the question. How could I have been so blind?

When I finished a few minutes later, I made my way off the stage while the emcee introduced the next speaker. As I entered the lobby in search of coffee, Rachel sauntered up.

"Nice job up there!"

"Thanks," I said as she caught up to me and joined me at the coffee station. "Pretty good crowd for an early Tuesday morning."

"Well, your opening joke had them rolling. I didn't even have to fake my laughter this time," she said.

"Very kind of you," I said, giving her a smirk. "I was a bit thrown by that one question, though. The one about measuring PVTV. I'm surprised we never thought of that."

Rachel made herself some tea, and we made our way over to a few seats close to the window.

"I guess, but do you think that's really needed? We've been doing well with PVTV for years and never found the need to measure it," she said.

"True, but it does make me wonder how much stronger we'd be if we *were* gauging our progress against it. And maybe we haven't needed it quite as much because we are kind of a startup, so there's more of an inherent belief in what we're doing?"

I was more asking a question than making a statement. As I was about to pursue the thought, an alert popped up on my phone. It was time for me to leave for a client meeting.

"Okay, well, I guess that's food for thought. I need to head out," I said, standing up. "Are you hanging around for the rest of the conference?"

"Of course. I can't leave Eric and his team members here all alone!" she said. "Plus, I'm really curious to hear the closing keynote by Jack Stack. He wrote *The Great Game of Business*. I've heard great things about that system for running a company."

"Sounds good. Let me know how that goes. Tell Eric I'm sorry I couldn't stay, and I'll see ya back at the shop," I said.

I requested Lyft to pick me up, entering the SalesLive address as my destination. While I waited, my mind quickly went back to the idea of measuring PVTV. I needed to bounce the thought off of Charles to see what he thought. After all, he had been the one to introduce me to the concept. And, come to think of it, he was the one who told me, "what gets measured gets done." Had he missed something so obvious as well?

SECTION ONE: PURPOSE, VISION, TENETS & VALUES (PVTV)

SalesLive was one of our longest-standing clients and one of the most successful tech startups in our city. Over the past few years, they had swelled to over 400 employees. Their growth was due mainly to great product-market fit (people wanted their offering), a growing industry (sales), and a CEO who just wouldn't stop (Shera).

Shera had asked for a meeting, which wasn't out of the ordinary. It was the vagueness of her ask that had me curious. I had checked with Steve (our head of customer relationships) if there was anything I needed to know about the working relationship, and he assured me everything was going great.

Due to their monolithic growth, SalesLive had once again moved into new office space. This time, they had pulled out all the stops. As I approached the reception desk, I was greeted by a robot. It looked like an evolution of Rosey from The Jetsons, only shinier and without the Brooklyn accent.

"Hello and welcome to SalesLive," she said, sounding so human it caught me off guard. "How can I help you today?"

"Good morning," I said, feeling silly immediately but no less amazed. "I'm here to see Shera. We have a 10:30 a.m. appointment."

An audible "Hmmmmm" came from the robot, stalling as her processor searched for the meeting in her database. "I found it. Your name must be William, is that correct?"

"Well, my friends call me Will. Only my mother calls me William, and that's only when I've done something bad," I said.

She was motionless for a second, then looked up at me. Her robot eyes blinked a few times. After a few more seconds of awkward tension, I sighed and said, "Yes, I'm William."

"Great! Please have a seat." She pointed to a couch.

I took my seat and, watching the people moving through the lobby, immediately became painfully aware of how much older I was. I'm not sure I saw a person younger than 30 years old—and they were all moving with a sense of urgency. Several of them gave Rosey a high-five. One of them even asked her, "What's shaking?" to which she replied, "Ain't no thang, but a chicken wang," which made me sure she could understand what I said about my mom calling me William. Rude.

As I was about to try connecting with her again (this time, I'd compliment her shine), Shera called my name and waved for me to come.

As I passed Rosey, I attempted to high-five her. There's nothing more humiliating than a grown man holding his hand out to high-five a robot that just looks at him and blinks, expressionless.

I shrugged and made my way to Shera, and after we greeted each other with a hug, she said, "Don't take it personally. She can be a bit temperamental."

Laughing, I followed her down the hall.

The hall led to a massive open space, with people on scooters zooming across the room, groups of people huddled together at a whiteboard wall, and desks neatly organized in groups of four and six. As always, the energy at SalesLive was off the charts.

She led me toward the back of the building, where we ended up at a small conference area set back from the rest of the mayhem. It wasn't a room exactly, but more like an area with a few rolling whiteboards pulled together to make it seem more secluded and private.

We grabbed seats at the small table, and I asked, "So, how're things?"

"Things are great! I've never felt better about the state of the business. We're beating our quarterly numbers consistently, and in a month or so, we're going to launch an entirely new product line."

"That's so great! I'm always impressed with how fast your company grows. And how's the implementation of PVTV going?"

Almost a year ago, Shera had approached me about explaining the PVTV concept to her as a possible way to create unity within her company as it continued to grow. She had been starting to see signs of disconnection from the company's core. Based on what I had told her about Matt's and RedBrick's success with the model, she wanted to know more.

After 30 minutes, she was sold and took the idea to her team. Over the next month, they created their company's PVTV on their own, with a few texts back and forth between Shera and me to keep them on track. I had been very impressed (though not surprised) that she could do that without more consulting help from me.

"Oh, we live by PVTV now! I actually talked about it recently with one of my team members. Even though I've succeeded in corporate America and as an entrepreneur with SalesLive, I'd always felt like something was missing. I could never quite put my finger on it, but I knew there was an important piece of the puzzle that had eluded me.

"That is until you told me about PVTV," she said. "What I was failing to see was that we didn't have a unifying purpose bringing us together as a team. Even though I was up in front of the staff every week, sharing our progress and revving them up, we were honestly a bit rudderless without PVTV."

"It's wild how simply having a structured, formalized foundation like PVTV can bring everything together, isn't it? The same thing happened to me when Charles first made me aware of it," I said.

"How's Charles doing, anyway? You know, I have to say, he must be the world's best investor. He wrote his check at the beginning, responds kindly to my updates, always answers when I reach out to him for advice. Otherwise, he lets me do what I need to do," she said. "He once told me that his job is to give me whatever help I need, but mainly, it's to get out of the way and watch me go."

Charles had been one of the first investors in Shera's business and had been the one to introduce us. A great mentor does that kind of thing.

"Oh yeah, he's the best. Right now, I believe he's on another epic cycling trip around Europe. I hope to catch up with him soon, and I'll be sure to tell him you asked about him," I said. "So, what can I help you with?"

She got up and began pacing back and forth as she explained.

"You know how I mentioned that we have a new product line that we're launching in about a month? Well, the team that is over that initiative is . . . struggling a bit," she said.

"How so?" I asked.

She shrugged her shoulders and said, "Honestly, I can't figure it out. I put one of my best leaders on it, Megan Scott. She's been here for years and has always performed, and I put together a team of aces for her, but they're a bit dysfunctional if you ask me."

I remembered meeting Megan in a brainstorming meeting that my agency had done for SalesLive. If memory served, she was one of the team's more active and engaged members.

Before I could jump in, she said, "And it's not a Peter Principle thing. She's done this role before. In fact, she's always been my best team leader."

Shera seemed to anticipate that I had been about to ask about the Peter Principle. It states that a person will rise in an organization to the level of their incompetence. Someone great at a particular role often will get regularly promoted until they reach a level where they don't succeed any longer. They become an enigma, someone who used to be great and is now struggling. It can be an easy trap for companies, especially growing ones, to fall into.

"And this launch is important, I'm guessing?" I asked, knowing the answer.

"Of course! It's a huge new initiative that we're betting big on. I'm not sure what to do, so I guess I wanted to meet with you to get your advice. Should I pull her off the project and put someone else in?"

"Do you have any other leaders that you think could do the role?"

"Well, I have a few who would be okay, but none of them are quite the right fit. Megan is a blend of diligence and creativity, which makes her perfect for this assignment. Plus, we're pretty slammed right now, so pulling someone off of what they're working on would be very disruptive."

I thought for a moment about the problem. Megan had been a terrific team member and had successfully run teams before. What was different this time?

"Has Megan worked under the pressure of a tight deadline before?" I asked.

Laughing, Shera said, "Will, we're always under a tight deadline here. And while we have a hard deadline for this launch, the amount of work to get done isn't out of alignment with the time allotted for it."

Then it hit me.

"In the past, when Megan performed, how were her teams formed?"

Shera thought for a second. "She's run two teams, and both were formed organically over time. In both cases, as the product they were working on grew, so did the team. She chose people she had worked with before."

Now we were getting somewhere.

"And with this team, it sounds like you picked the team for her, and they're all high-performing, A-players, right?" I asked.

"That's right." She paused. "Wait, do you think that's the problem? Should I let her change up the team?"

"I'm not sure that's the *problem*, per se. But I would bet anything that's contributing to the dysfunction and her struggle. Plus, I'm guessing you chose those team members for her because you know they have the skills needed for a successful product launch?"

"Correct again. So what do you suggest?"

"Tell you what, how about if I meet with Megan and see if I can figure out how to get her back on track? I'd be happy to spend time with her to understand more from her perspective what the challenges are. Maybe between the two of us, we will figure something out. I do love tackling a good problem," I said.

"Oh, I know you do," she said, then added, "Okay, but we need to set that meeting up as quickly as possible because there's no time to waste."

"Deal," I said. "If you would connect us via email, I'll have my admin send her some times that work for us to meet at my office tomorrow."

She pulled out her phone and quickly fired off the email. "Done," she said.

Walking back through the office to the exit, I looked up at the massive wall in the main area. Someone had drawn SalesLive's PVTV across the whole wall for everyone to see. I quickly snapped a pic to share with my team, because we're always on the lookout for the unique ways that companies bring their PVTV to life.

The Lyft dropped me off in front of our office. Getting out of the car, I looked up at the 25-floor building, trying to locate the 17th floor, where my team had our office space. We'd moved in several years before and had continued to add square footage as we grew. I made my way through the lobby and entered the elevator bank for floors 17–25. Just as the doors were closing, Rachel stuck her hand in, then joined me in the elevator.

"Just getting back from SalesLive?"

"Hey, Rach," I said. "No, I ended up swinging by The Steaming Cup first to get some writing done."

The Steaming Cup was my favorite coffee spot. I often found pockets of time throughout the week to park in my favorite booth and work on my writing. My writing consisted of a weekly email newsletter accompanied by a blog post and some social media posts. Mostly I write about leadership and purpose-driven leaders and companies. The practice of writing is my preferred form of meditation and a great way to organize my thoughts.

We reached our stop, and our receptionist greeted us when we entered.

"Hey, Will. Hey, Rachel," said Billy. "Rachel, you have some mail here."

Billy was a young man who had come to us as an intern from the local university in our town. We had a long history of team members who worked the front desk, eventually moving their way up in the organization as they gained experience. It was something I had learned at the first startup I worked at, Crackersnap, where a young receptionist named Misty eventually made her way to the head of operations. I had high hopes for Billy.

As Rachel grabbed the stack of mail and thumbed through it, she shot me a sideways glance, "Bills, bills, and oh, more bills. This is why you promoted me to president, right?"

"Well," I deadpanned, "it's not the *only* reason."

The lobby featured large comfy chairs and a stack of industry magazines on a chic table. Just beyond it was our large conference room. We usually reserved it for leadership team meetings, board meetings, big client meetings, and pitches. It was currently full of people.

"What's going on in there?" I asked Rachel.

"The creative team is working through some issues. I was getting complaints from some of their team members and some other teams about how the creative team was behaving. I finally told them to just get in the same room and hash it out. I decided the big conference room was the best place for them to do that."

There did seem to be some heated exchanges going on in the conference room.

"You think it'll work?" I asked.

"Doubt it, but I always prefer they work things out on their own if possible," she said. "Oh, you had asked about the conference. I did get to spend some good time with Eric and his team, but the best part was the talk that Jack Stack gave at the closing keynote."

"You mean, the 'second-best part'?" I teased. "As I recall, you did attend *my* keynote."

"Weeeellllllll . . . ," she said, laughing.

We were getting close to our desks, which were near the center of one of the larger open areas. Our office was set up similarly to SalesLive, with mostly open spaces. The difference was that our office had tremendous views of the city, whereas Shera's office was in a warehouse in a trendy part of the city. She had brick walls with graffiti, and we had views stretching out miles over the landscape.

"All jokes aside, what was great about Jack's talk?" I asked.

She sat at her desk, which faced mine. "I'll have to tell you about it later, but the entire concept of *The Great Game of Business* is really intriguing. It might be something for us to consider at some point."

The next morning I woke up early and crept out of bed as silently as I could in an effort not to wake up my wife, Sarah. My ninja-like stealth was on point as I made my way to the bathroom, softly landing each foot on the hardwood floor. Both Sarah and our daughter, Danielle, had told me that I stomped around the house like an elephant.

Not this morning, ladies.

Using the glow from my watch to guide me through the dark room, I was almost to safety when I stepped on one of Danielle's Barbie Convertibles. (I swear it was not there when we went to bed.) I slipped on the car and became airborne. I landed on my back, on top of the same toy that caused the fall. It was a historically awkward feat.

CRASH!

"Will, is that you?" Sarah said, sitting up quickly in bed wearing a confused look on her face.

Groaning, I said, "Yes. Sorry, honey. Please go back to bed. I can call the ambulance myself."

She flipped on the light next to the bed and peered down at me. "What are you doing down there?"

I chuckled, "Just cleaning up some toys. Sorry to wake you." I worked to find the feeling in my legs again so I could stand up.

I guess ninjas don't have six-year-old girls.

Fifteen minutes later, I'd had a quick shower and was on my way downstairs to the kitchen. I started the coffee and pulled out my laptop. Charles and I had agreed to connect at 5:00 a.m. because he was in Edinburgh and only had a small window for us to talk.

I checked some emails while I waited for the coffee and saw a note from Megan Scott at SalesLive. It read:

Will,

Per Shera's email, I would be thrilled if you could take some time to try to help me. I could come to your office any time this afternoon. Please let me know if I need to bring anything with me.

Megan

Looking through my calendar, I fired back a quick response:

Megan,

Great, I'm excited to meet up. If it works for you, I can meet from 3-4:00 p.m. this afternoon.

And no need to bring anything besides an open mind :)

See you then,
Will

Immediately after I hit send, I heard a ping from my laptop indicating that Charles had entered the video chat.

"Will, are you there?" I heard Charles asking as my laptop began connecting.

"Yes, Charles, I'm here," I said as the video component of the chat came online. I could see that Charles was on his phone, and the background was quite incredible. He appeared to be just on the outskirts of what I imagined to be Edinburgh (I had never been), and I saw some other people on bikes behind him.

"Great. Sorry about the early morning for you! It's close to noon here, and we're about to head off on a ride through the Highlands. It's meant to be beautiful country up there. And if we're lucky, we'll be at Loch Ness in two days."

"Well, be careful. I heard there's a monster up there that's partial to attacking cyclists," I said.

"What's that, Will? Sorry, you broke up for a second. Did you say something about being attacked? Is everything okay?"

"No, sorry, I was just making a joke. And no worries on the early call, you know I'm an early bird. Plus I'm eager to get your thoughts about something," I said.

He nodded and said, "Lay it on me."

I told him about the question the young man had asked me at the end of my keynote yesterday and the nagging feeling that we had missed something when it came to measuring PVTV.

"That *is* interesting. In all my years of practicing PVTV and then the additional years of sharing it with others, I never thought about the idea of actually measuring it. It seems wild given how much I have held to the idea that what gets measured gets done," he said. "Let me ask you something. Besides the feeling that we should measure it, has there been anything you've seen that would indicate that a formal way of gauging the impact of PVTV would help make it more impactful? Are there any problems that have arisen either with your shop or others you've coached on PVTV?"

"I'm not sure what you mean, exactly. What kind of issues might there be from a lack of measurement?" I asked.

He paused for a minute to speak with one of the other cyclists, then said, "Will, my time is running short here. Sorry about that. Let's talk again sometime later next week. I should be in Ireland by then and will have some downtime. Here's what I'd like you to do in the meantime. Remember, when we measure something, we find ways to work on it. And when done across an entire team or company, measurement allows everyone to know how they can impact the goals and even create new ones. As you know, with PVTV, the idea isn't to develop specific goals but to create a foundation for building a purpose-driven, meaningful business.

"I suppose people can begin to feel disconnected without measurement in place. They might be unsure of how to impact their PVTV, and you might see in-fighting or lack of team unity. If you find problems like that, you might just find the answer to your question," he said.

I saw him wave to someone in front of him and give them a thumbs up. He said, "Okay, sorry again, but I do have to leave now. Otherwise, they'll leave me behind. I hope that was helpful. Let's connect next week and see what you've come up with."

"Thanks as always, and enjoy the ride!" I said, and we hung up.

I needed to look for problems creeping up with teams using PVTV. My first thought was to check with Matt to see how they were doing at Titan. Maybe he'd seen something similar. I sent him a text to ask if he'd be up for lunch on Friday. We were overdue for a catch-up anyway. As soon as I hit send, I heard small footsteps coming down the stairs.

Our six-year-old, Danielle, came softly into the room. She was the picture of cuteness: hair messy from the night's sleep, pink pajamas with pandas on them, her eyes squinting at me through the bright light of the kitchen.

"Daddy, was that Uncle Charles?" she asked as she made her way toward me.

"Oh, sorry baby, I hope we didn't wake you. Yes, that was Uncle Charles. He's over in Scotland right now, and we had to have an early morning call," I said, pulling her in close.

Rubbing her eyes, she said, "Okay. You and Uncle Charles didn't wake me up. I heard a big bang. Did we have an earthquake?"

"Oh, you heard that, did you? Let's just say that your Barbie Convertible wasn't made for an elephant attack."

Later that afternoon, I found myself thinking eagerly about the meeting with Megan. I wanted to get her to open up and needed her to do it quickly. We only had an hour, and her team was under a tight deadline. I decided on my favorite type of meeting: the walk-and-talk.

Years ago, I learned about this method of conversation from a business leader. She had shared with me that the easiest way to have a difficult conversation, in business or otherwise, is by walking together. It was famously Steve Jobs's favorite way to have meetings.

She explained that something interesting happens when we don't force ourselves to look each other in the eyes. It allows people to speak more freely. And the energy that comes from the fresh air, exercise, and small distractions when we walk outside allow for a more engaging conversation.

I tried the method and loved it right away. One difference was that I used it for many types of meetings, not just difficult ones. In most cases, people were more creative and open-minded when walking and talking. And that kind of thinking was exactly what I would need to get the most out of my meeting with Megan.

I swung by the lobby ten minutes before Megan was due to arrive to let Billy know to expect her and found her already sitting in one of the big chairs. She was in her early 30s and a graduate of one of the best universities in the area. According to her bio on the SalesLive website, she was an avid half-marathoner and skier.

Well-educated, hard working, and on time to the point of being early—I could see why Shera had high hopes for her.

"Hey, Megan. Thanks for coming by," I said as I approached.

She grinned at me and grabbed her notebook as she stood. "Hi, Will, great to see you again! Thanks again for taking the time. I really appreciate it."

We shook hands, and I said, "Remind me, have you been to our office before? I know we've been in meetings at your office, but I can't remember if you've ever visited us."

She shook her head. "No, this is my first time. I can barely get over these views!"

"Up for a quick tour?"

"Of course!"

I led her out of the lobby and into the main area. I always gave tours of our space by walking our guests past the windows, both so they could see the incredible views and get a better sense of the office.

As we made our way through, she noticed a large amount of writing on the windows.

"At our space, we have whiteboards all over the place, but I notice here, your team seems to prefer writing on the windows!" she said.

"Yeah, it's funny. I never expected that to be the case, but when we first moved in, the type of whiteboard we wanted was out of stock, and team members often congregated near the windows because of the views. On day one, that's all it took. Someone grabbed a dry erase marker and started to outline an idea. And ever since then, that's the way we operate," I said.

"I suppose it's a bonus that you don't have whiteboards separating the rooms the way we do. Plus, you saved a lot of money by not buying them!" she added.

"Correct. Sometimes you have to let a team work before you spot a solution. If those whiteboards had been in stock, we never would have realized this better way of operating. Plus, it looks pretty cool, doesn't it?" I said with a smile.

As we continued the tour, Megan said, "I once read about a university that was debating where to put the sidewalks when they were architecting their campus. One of the engineering professors suggested they hold off on putting in any sidewalks for a month. By that time, the students would have walked the paths between buildings that made the most sense for them. Their patterns would wear down the grass, and that would answer where to put the sidewalks."

"That's brilliant!" I said. "What a smart way to solve a problem."

I was impressed that she was spending time reading articles like that. It signaled to me that she was someone who studied the craft of leadership and planning. Not everyone has that trait. The more I got to know her, the more confused I was that she was struggling.

As we circled back to the lobby, I asked her if she was up for a walk instead of sitting in a stuffy conference room. She agreed, and we made our way down the elevators.

Just across the street from our building was Foothills Park. It was a smaller yet arguably more beautiful version of New York's Central Park. Foothills was in the center of the city and contained a small lake, many fields and playgrounds, dozens of great paths, and a small petting zoo.

We started off headed west along the path that circled the park. After a little chit-chat, I decided it was time to get down to business.

"So, Shera says that you're having some issues with your new team. Is that right?"

"Yes, you could say that," she said. "I don't know what's happening, but I can't seem to get them on the same page. It's really frustrating!"

"How long has the team been together?" I asked.

She thought for a moment and said, "A little over a month. And I think we've spent more time arguing than getting any actual work done."

I could tell by her body language that she was a bit dispirited.

"Megan, I know from what Shera said that you've been very successful with your past teams, and that's excellent. But you should know that having problems within a team is extremely common. Actually, it's more common than not. So don't beat yourself up about it. You've just set the bar too high in terms of initial team chemistry, but we're going to figure out how to get you back on track, don't worry."

She smiled and said, "Okay, that does make me feel better. Where do we start?"

"Let's start by describing some of the things that people on the team are arguing about," I said.

We were rounding a corner near a small pond, and some kids ran in front of us chasing a soccer ball. After the last kid crossed, we continued our walk.

"I can tell you what the problem was this morning. We had a big debate about the main focus of our team. A few people argued that our top priority is quality. No matter what, we need to ensure the new product is of the highest possible quality," she said.

"That sounds reasonable. What was the other side arguing for?"

"The others were convinced that our top priority was customer activation. They said that it didn't matter how great our product was if our customers didn't sign up for the new service."

"Hard to argue with that either," I said.

"Oh, and that wasn't it. There was a third group . . . well, really just one person, but she was convinced that, above all else, the new offering had to attract new customers."

"Wow, that also sounds like a good objective," I said. "You're a month into this project with a little over a month to go, and your team isn't aligned on the goal?"

She sighed. "Yes, that's correct."

"What does Shera say when you bring her problems like this?" I asked.

"Shera is so slammed that I haven't brought her much. Plus, I want to solve this myself and prove to her she didn't make a mistake by choosing me," she said.

That made sense, but also, I thought it was a mistake. Had Shera not asked me to get involved, I wonder if Megan would have sought anyone's advice. Without working on this problem, the project could have sunk. I've certainly learned the hard way that pride can be a tricky thing.

"Let's back up," I said. "I know that you run PVTV at your company. What is a company's Purpose?"

She thought for a minute and said, "I believe it is their reason for being. It's meant to be larger in scope than their Vision, which is the company they wish to become, right?"

"Bingo, you nailed it," I said. "And what about the Tenets and Values?"

"The Tenets are the ways that a company will achieve its Vision. And the Values are the behaviors you want to exhibit. Basically, these are the way you should behave," she said.

"Correct again! And what's SalesLive's Purpose?" I asked.

"It's to eliminate the tension between salespeople and their prospects," she said.

I was astonished that she knew SalesLive's Purpose word for word. I had printed out their PVTV, expecting I would have to remind her of what they were.

"Wow, terrific that you remember it!" I said.

"Oh, yeah, well, I've always been an A student, you know? When Shera said she wanted everyone to memorize our Purpose, Vision, Tenets & Values, I made sure that I did. Would you like to know the rest?" she asked.

"You know I do!"

"Okay, here we go." Her eyes looked up at the sky, and I could tell she was digging into her memory to call up the words. "Our Vision is to be the ultimate tool for our customers to achieve their sales goals. We will do this by putting the customer first, believing in each other, and focusing on profitable growth. Those are our Tenets. And we believe in being all for one and one for all, gaining advantage, and always being two steps ahead. Those are our Values."

Again, I was stunned by her dedication to memorizing their PVTV.

"Megan, that's super impressive! Have you tried going back to those words to see if you can use them to align the team?" I asked.

"It's funny you mention that. I was reading your book, *The 5-Day Turnaround*, a few weeks back, and there is a part where you suggest doing just that. I did give it a try, but I kept feeling like the words were too generic for our team. Like, I get how they work for SalesLive, but I don't see how they fit within our team given the very specific assignment we have," she said.

She seemed bummed by her inability to use PVTV to right the ship. I pulled out the written PVTV and read through it.

Indeed, I could see her point. Looking at these words through her eyes—"putting the customer first," "believing in each other," and "focusing on profitable growth" were solid concepts for the Vision of SalesLive. They just weren't going to direct her team as well as they'd guide the company.

As I was processing this, something I had recently read came to mind.

"I'm reading a John F. Kennedy biography, and there's a story in there about JFK touring NASA's headquarters in 1961. He sees a janitor mopping the floor and asks him what he does at NASA."

"The janitor looks up at the President and says, proudly, 'Why, I'm putting a man on the moon!'"

Continuing, I said, "I've been thinking about that quite a bit lately. Here was this janitor, not by any stretch a senior person at NASA, doing the dirty work of cleaning up, and yet he knew he was there to help put a man on the moon. Clearly, he believed in NASA's overall mission and was able to see how he was contributing to it."

"I love that story. And I do think that what our team is doing will help eliminate the tension between salespeople and their customers. In fact, that's exactly what our new product aims to do," she said.

"Okay, so let's think about the janitor's story. I'm guessing that if NASA was running PVTV, their Tenets might be something like, 'Ensure premium quality' and 'Efficiency at the highest level.'"

"And probably one like, 'Trust in your team.' I've read about NASA, and apparently, it only works through complete trust amongst everyone," she added.

"Exactly. That's perfect. Now let's think about those through the lens of the janitor. As he tries to do his job, does it help him to 'ensure premium quality'?"

She thought for a second and said, "I think that one works pretty well, right? He's in charge of the quality of the cleanliness and needs to make sure everything is sanitary and organized so that the rest of the team can work."

"I buy that. What about the one about efficiency?" I asked.

"I'm not sure that one fits as easily. And now that I think of it, even though trust in the team is important, it probably doesn't help the custodial team too much," she said.

We were getting close to completing the loop, and our hour was almost up. I had already realized what the correct answer was for Megan, but I was hoping she would get there on her own.

"So how would you suggest the janitor work through problems on his team if the PVTV doesn't match up well for them specifically?" I asked.

She picked up a large leaf off of the ground and began shredding it as she thought. "I guess I'd suggest that he try to find a way for PVTV to work for his team without conflicting with the overall PVTV for NASA. Is that possible?"

"What do you think? Remember the story I told in *The 5-Day Turnaround* about the way PVTV came to life?" I asked.

"Sure, you helped a marketing team create their own PVTV. But you made sure it wasn't in conflict with the company's overall purpose, which I recall wasn't fully developed." She paused thoughtfully. "So you think we could have a PVTV for our team, even though our company has one already?"

"You bet! I don't think it's always necessary, but I would expect as companies grow, more and more teams will need to find a unique foundation—their own reason for being. And I think that's what you need to do, and I'd be thrilled to help," I said as we exited the park.

As we crossed the street and went into my building, I shared a similar model that had helped me with Matt at Titan. We could get together each Monday for four weeks. Each meeting would focus on a component of PVTV. Along the way, they'd work through ways to bring that element to life. By the end of our sessions (which fit nicely with their project timeline), they'd have worked through their issues and would be the rockstar team they were meant to be.

We checked out calendars in the lobby, locked down the best times, and said our good-byes. As she left, I started thinking about the clients I had worked with to implement PVTV. About half were for their company overall, with the other half being for a specific team. I had never helped a team create a PVTV when their company already had one in place.

Good thing I was meeting Matt for lunch on Friday. I heard they were doing the same thing at Titan.

Friday morning, I woke up early, this time avoiding any Barbie-traps, and made my way out for a morning run. My current workout plan was to do at least two short runs a week, usually around three or four miles, and always in the morning. Then, on the weekend, I'd grab a long run whenever I could make it work, usually five miles or more.

It was a bit chilly when I took off, but I warmed up by the first mile. I was listening to a podcast and letting my mind wander.

Most likely because I would see Matt at lunch, I started to think about our time together at Crackersnap. There was one late night when the CEO, Matt, and I were the last ones in the office. It was just after midnight, and we had officially pushed our new service offering live. We sent the rest of the team home and decided to celebrate with a much-needed beer.

"Well, boys," Stan said, "we did it. Six months of hard work, persistence, and a little bit of luck, and we're here."

"I still can't believe it," Matt said. "I never thought we'd hit the deadline after so many setbacks, but you kept telling the team we could do it, and sure enough, we did!"

We cheered our beers and exchanged happy, exhausted smiles.

"You know, that's the good stuff," Stan said.

"What, *this*?" I asked, looking at my beer. "I think these are past their expiration date."

"No, not the beer, Will," he laughed. "The journey!"

"What do you mean?" Matt asked.

"I think it was Andy Rooney, an old broadcaster that I'm sure you two have never heard of, who said, 'Everyone wants to live on top of the mountain, but all the happiness and growth occurs while you're climbing it.' And you know what, he's right. It's amazing to be where we are right now, having climbed to the top of the mountain."

"But all the great memories, all that perseverance, all the sweat and tears . . . that's the good stuff. That's what makes it all worth it, and years from now, when we're all off on different adventures, that's the bit we'll remember."

Thinking back on it, he had never been more right. I could remember the next-to-impossible problems we solved, the arguments we had, how individuals stepped up and realized their full potential amid chaos. There were many significant points along the journey that felt even better than achieving the goal.

The journey is the good stuff.

Naan Place was my favorite lunch spot. It was walkable from my office but out of the way enough to keep most people from being aware of it. It was quiet, making it perfect for lunch meetings. Plus, the food was delicious.

I arrived early and sat down in my favorite booth. There was only one other table occupied, with what looked to be a young couple. I took a look at the menu as I waited, but I knew what I would order. In fact, I was pretty sure even the waiter knew my order.

Matt came in right on time. He spotted me easily and strode over. Sitting down, he said, "Creature of habit, huh?"

"Yep, you know me," I nodded. "When I find something good, I stick with it."

The server came over and took our drink orders. After she left, Matt said, "Man, why didn't you ever tell me being a CEO was so much . . . work!"

I laughed. "So, what's going on? I hope it's not Eric-related," I said, half-joking. I knew Eric could march to his own beat at times, but ever since Matt had promoted him to chief growth officer, I'd only heard good things.

"Nope, not Eric-related," he said. "Though I did talk with him. He said you crushed it at the conference. I wish I could have been there." Matt paused and ran his hand through his hair. "Will, I feel like somehow the business is off track. It's like, somehow, half our company doesn't seem to be as into it as they were when I took over."

"That was when, about six months ago?" I asked.

"Yep, just about on the dot. And for the first few months, things were going so well. As you remember, we implemented PVTV across the company, using the methods you helped me deploy with the marketing team. Thanks to you, we call them the growth team now. I still can't believe we pulled that off, by the way," he said.

"You're telling me! I think I barely slept for a month during that period. And who knew it would launch both of us into essentially completely new careers!"

"Quite an experience. Anyway, things were going great, and then, about three months ago, I started noticing cracks in the armor. There were little things here and there. Nothing was a big deal on its own, but those little problems add up. And now, I think I'm on the edge of the whole thing unraveling completely!"

I was sure he was over-dramatizing, but still, I didn't like what I was hearing.

The server brought our drinks, and as suspected, correctly assumed what I'd be having. Come to think of it, the barista at The Steaming Cup and I were on a first-name basis, and she always knew my order. Maybe I did need a little spontaneity in my life?

"So, what do you think?" Matt asked, waking me out of my introspection.

"If you had to pinpoint an overarching theme for the problems, what would it be?" I asked.

He sat back and thought about it for a minute. He finally sighed and said, "I guess, if I had to, I would say there was a feeling of discontent. Like a lack of a feeling that we're all in it together, and maybe people aren't feeling appreciated or seeing themselves as part of the team."

That sounded familiar. Hadn't Rachel recently used some of those words to describe some of the problems she saw at our shop?

"And the PVTV you created for the company isn't aligning people enough?" I asked, a bit puzzled.

"I thought it would, and I've continued to push into it over the last few months as I've seen these problems, but it doesn't seem to be having the effect I want. I think people get it. They understand why we exist and what we're trying to accomplish, but . . ." he paused as he searched for the right words. "But I guess maybe they don't see how they fit into it, exactly. I suppose that's the difference between the PVTV we had—still have, actually—for the growth team. It was a small enough team that everyone felt really connected to it, whereas with the size we are at Titan, I'm not sure that's happening."

"You know, I'm not sure I have a great answer to that just yet. But as it happens, I think the same thing might be happening at my agency. Rachel mentioned something similar. I wonder if, with our growth, we're seeing some of the same signs. You mind if I think about that for a bit?" I asked.

"No problem, I just hope you can help me once again!" He said with a laugh, just as our food arrived.

As we ate, we talked about how my agency was performing. After a bit, I jumped into the real thing I wanted to discuss.

"You're still allowing Eric and the growth team to run their own version of PVTV, correct?"

He dipped some naan into the tzatziki and said, "Oh yeah, he's still rocking and rolling with the original PVTV!"

"Interesting. I guess I assumed when a company had an overall PVTV, its teams wouldn't need their own. And you've found no problem with that conflicting with the overall company PVTV?"

"Not at all. I mean, Eric gets how to manage the PVTV because he was a part of it with us in the beginning. And when we created the company-wide one, we used Eric's team as an example. Actually, I feel pretty good about all the teams that are running their PVTVs."

"What? More teams are using this model in the company?" I asked, a bit stunned.

He looked at me like I was crazy. "Will, I couldn't have stopped them if I had wanted to. Think about it, we implemented PVTV in our team, and soon after, we were kicking all sorts of butt. Everyone was looking at us, trying to figure out what we had done. And then on top of everything else, I was promoted to CEO! I think Eric and I have probably stood up more PVTVs than you have at this point."

I laughed and thought that he might not be wrong.

"Maybe I'll get you to ghostwrite my next book then," I said with a chuckle.

"Not interested, I'll leave the writing to you. Why are you curious about the PVTVs in our company?"

"You remember Shera from SalesLive?" I asked. He nodded, and I explained her issue.

"I think there's a good chance that Megan's team needs a PVTV of its own."

He looked at me with an expression that I could only describe as, "Well, duh."

"Okay, Mr. Expert, let me ask you one more thing then," I said. "Do the teams that run a unique PVTV have the same Purpose and Values as the overall company? I know they have a distinct Vision and Tenets, but what about Purpose and Values?"

"Some do, and some don't," Matt said. "Some have a specific Purpose but kept the Values, some vice versa, and some changed them both. I have a few teams that completely kept the company's Purpose and Values without changing a word. As long as I approve them to make sure they're in alignment with the company's PVTV, I'm good with it."

The server came by and set the bill folder down next to me. Matt went to grab it, but I showed him that this was actually the receipt.

"Sorry, pal. I gave him my card the moment I got here. Your money's no good here," I said, laughing.

"Thanks for the advice," I said, as we started to get up. "And at some point, I need to come by and see all these rogue PVTVs running through your office!"

"No worries, and you're welcome any time. Your team is over

almost daily, as you know. But listen, I'll give you all the advice you want if you help me figure out how to get things back on track at Titan. I'll be waiting to hear what you come up with," he said.

We said our good-byes, and Matt headed to the parking lot. I turned the other way and started the walk back to my office.

I shouldn't have been surprised that Matt had taken PVTV and made it work for him in ways I had never imagined. I did, after all, help him remember his old entrepreneurial self during Titan's five-day turnaround.

Looking at my phone, I checked my calendar and saw that I had no more meetings the rest of the day. That was good because I needed to prepare for my meeting with Megan and her team on Monday morning.

PURPOSE

I tossed and turned all night. It was something I did every time I had a "big day" ahead. But just like when I'd met with Matt so many months before, I sprang out of bed in the morning, excited about the meeting with Megan's team.

The weekend had been full. In between activities like taking Danielle to the park with Sarah, having my in-laws over for dinner, church on Sunday morning, and going on a run, I'd worked a decent amount to prepare for this day. And no matter what we were doing, I was thinking about how it would go.

In the middle of our dinner with Sarah's parents, I had an idea. I excused myself from the table, swiftly grabbed my phone, and hid out in the bathroom to furiously type a note about the concept.

"Busted," Sarah said as we were washing dishes later. "I thought it was weird that you excused yourself to use the restroom in the middle of dinner."

"Ah, yeah, sorry," I said. "If your mom asks, just tell her it was her potato salad."

She gave me a light shove and just shook her head.

I arrived at the SalesLive office for the second time in two weeks. I made my way into the lobby and, once again, found myself face to face with Rosey, my robotic arch-nemesis.

"Hi there, I'm, uh, here to see Megan. Megan Scott," I said, oddly nervous about this innocuous interaction.

She looked up at me, blinking, and said, "Welcome back, William. It is good to see you again." I could swear she rolled her eyes.

Continuing, she said, "I will tell Megan that you have arrived. Please take a seat over there." She pointed at the same couch I sat on last time.

"Thank you. And, if I do say so myself, you're looking lovely this morning," I said, trying to see if flattery would win her over.

Her eyes blinked many times, and then she said, "My programming does not allow me to have a relationship with our guests in that way. I hope you find what you are looking for somewhere else."

"Oh. No. I wasn't trying to have a . . . I just thought I'd . . . ," but before I could stammer anything more, she zoomed over to the other side of the room, spun around, and looked at me through a narrow split between her eyelids.

"Did I just get dissed by a robot?" I muttered to no one in particular.

After waiting for a few minutes, Megan came out and said, "Hi, Will, come on back. We're all ready for you."

Following her through the hallway and into the main area, I once again found the atmosphere exciting and energetic. People were moving this way and that, having small group huddles here and one-on-one chats there, all out in the open or in a semi-secluded, whiteboard-surrounded makeshift meeting area.

I took another look up at the PVTV painting on the main wall. At the top, just below the SalesLive logo, read:

Our Purpose is to eliminate the tension between salespeople and their prospects

That was what we'd be working on today.

Megan led us into one of the few conference rooms in their office. Five people were seated around the conference table. Megan motioned for me to sit at the head of the table.

"Okay, everyone," she said as I sat down, "I'll share why we're all here in a minute. But first, let's do introductions. Q, why don't you start?"

I quickly pulled out my notepad to take notes on who everyone was.

"I'm Qaadirah, but everyone calls me Q," she said. "I'm the lead product manager."

"Hi, Q," I said. "Nice to meet you."

"My name is Sasha," said the man to her right. "I'm in charge of delivery."

Sasha sounded like he might be from Germany.

Next was a woman named Hala (pronounced "hay-luh"). She was over technology.

"I'm Ashley, and this is Dustin," she said, motioning to the man sitting next to her. "We're the production leaders on the team. I'm over user experience, and Dustin leads creative."

"And I should add, if Ashley will let me speak for myself," Dustin said (in a playful way). "I love working with your team, Will. They're terrific."

"Thanks for saying that. I know the feeling is mutual!" I said. "Great to meet all of you, and I'm excited to be working with you."

"On that note, let me explain why we're all here," Megan said. "Will is going to help us come together as a team. I know that none of us are happy with how everything has been going since we all came together. And my guess is that you're as surprised as I am because we've all performed so well in the past."

I was looking around at everyone as she talked. Mostly head nods, so this wasn't surprising to them so far.

"Will spent some time talking with Shera, and then Will and I also talked last week. He generously offered to spend some time with us over the next month to help us create a PVTV for our team," she said.

Now they were surprised.

"What do you mean, our own PVTV?" asked Q.

Deciding it was time for me to enter the conversation, I jumped in, saying, "Megan, if it's all right, I'd like to back up just a bit."

"Sure! The floor is yours," she said.

"Thanks," I said. "Here's the way I see it. You're a team of rockstars. You've come together almost like a Navy SEAL team for a specific product launch. Shera chose you to bring this new, extremely important product to market in a decently tight timeframe. Any disagreements so far?"

"I like that. I suppose we'd be SEAL Team X because Shera is calling the product 'The X Factor,'" Hala said.

The team seemed to like this name. Ashley and Dustin even fist-bumped. So camaraderie wasn't necessarily the problem. That was interesting. And good.

Continuing, I said, "Only, so far, you're off to a rocky start. I hear you're on somewhat different pages about what you're trying to accomplish and how to get there."

More head nods.

"This lack of alignment and lack of a shared sense of belonging on a small team is usually corrected by a strong PVTV. But you all already have that. I see it every time I come into your office," I said, pointing toward the wall with the company PVTV.

"My theory is that, while your company's PVTV is powerful and guiding the business as a whole, it's not as helpful to your small team as it could be. Maybe the solution is for you to build your own," I said.

Sasha raised his hand.

I chuckled. "Please, everyone, you don't have to raise your hand." Then smiling at Sasha, I said, "Yes, Sasha?"

He smiled, putting his hand down. "Do other businesses have a PVTV for the company overall and then separate ones for individual teams?"

"You bet. In fact, I just had lunch with the CEO of Titan, and many of their teams have unique PVTVs. The trick is to make sure that all the individual team PVTVs coincide and lift the overall company's PVTV."

I got up and wrote on the whiteboard:

SalesLive Purpose

To eliminate the tension between salespeople and their prospects

SEAL Team X Purpose

??

"First, we need to decide if your team will need a distinct Purpose. Then, we'll work on Vision. You'll definitely need one that is unique to your team. Can someone other than Megan tell me why?" I asked.

Q was looking out the glass window toward the wall with their PVTV written on it. She said, "Well, the Vision of the company is to be the ultimate tool for our customers to achieve their sales goals. I guess we'd need our own because that's not exactly what our project is trying to do?"

Even though she answered with more questioning than confidence, she wasn't too far off.

"That's true! Your Vision is going to be a bit different from that. But does anyone know how we define the Vision of a team or company?"

I could see no one knew the answer other than Megan, who was fidgeting in her seat like the only kid in elementary school with the answer.

"Megan, why don't you give it a shot?"

"Thanks. Your Vision is the type of company or team you want to become. SalesLive wants to become the ultimate tool for our customers to achieve their sales goals. That makes sense—for the company. But our product, our piece of the overall business, isn't to become the ultimate tool. It's to serve a specific function," she said.

"Exactly," I said. "So, when we get to Vision, that is the first thing you all need to decide. What is the Vision for your team? What kind of team do you aspire to be? But we have to do some work to get there. For now, let's focus on Purpose. Megan, what's the difference between Purpose and Vision?"

"Purpose is the reason you exist. The change you want to make, essentially. Whereas Vision is the type of business you want to become," she said.

"Or type of team," added Dustin.

I continued to be impressed with how well Megan had grasped the concept of PVTV.

"Right again—and good add, Dustin," I said. "So the question we need to tackle first is, what is your team's Purpose? Is it okay to be the same as the company's?"

Sasha again raised his hand, then quickly caught himself and pulled it back down. "How do we decide that?" he asked.

I smiled. "Glad you asked. I have a few exercises that I'd like you to do to get to the answer."

I walked up to the whiteboard and wrote:

EXERCISE 1: Why + What

"Okay, the first thing you'll want to do as a group is to answer a lot of 'why' questions. Think about all the why's that pertain to your team. For instance, 'Why does your team exist?' and 'Why did Shera pick all of you to be on this team?'"

Continuing, I said, "And at the same time, you want to ask yourselves 'what' questions. 'What is your team trying to accomplish?' and 'What are your combined strengths?' Write any 'why' or 'what' question you can ask about this team on the board."

Some of the team members were making notes. I took it as a good sign.

"Once you have those questions, you can begin answering them as a team. Try to get to a good consensus on the answers, so you all feel good about them," I said.

I turned back to the whiteboard and wrote:

EXERCISE 2: 3 Rough Drafts Each

"After you've completed the first exercise, you're each going to write three possible Purpose statements. It's important you do these exercises in order. This part will take a few days. It's a critical part of the process."

Megan asked, "Do you have any guidelines on how to put a Purpose statement together?"

"Great question. I like to focus on a few things. First, a Purpose statement should be short and powerful. Second, it should be phrased as, 'Our Purpose is to' . . . then the statement. Third, it should be unattainable or close to it. Your Purpose is big, bold, and aspirational. It should inspire those who read it and give clarity to why your team exists."

"Could you give us a few examples, other than ours?" Sasha asked.

"Sure," I said.

I turned to the board and wrote:

PURPOSE STATEMENT EXAMPLES:

To inspire happiness through positive relationships, impactful work, and doing good.

To save our home planet.

To accelerate the world's transition to sustainable energy.

I looked around the room and asked, "Does anyone know what organizations own these Purpose statements?"

Dustin said, "Well, the first one is easy. That's your agency's Purpose! I know it because your team leads every presentation by reminding us." We all laughed.

"Right! And hopefully, the team is finding ways to inspire your happiness," I said. "What about the others? Any guesses?"

After a few attempts, someone guessed that the third one on sustainable energy was Tesla.

"The middle one there is one of my favorite purpose-driven brands, Patagonia. What I love about those two examples—Patagonia and Tesla—is that anyone who takes even a passing glance at these companies will see that they live their Purpose in everything they do," I said.

Sasha asked, "Are these the same exercises that you use when you help a company find its overall Purpose?"

"You bet. It's the same exact process," I said. "The big difference is, at the end of this process, it's okay if you decide that your team's Purpose is the same as the company's Purpose. In many cases, it will be. If you choose to create a Purpose just for your team, you'll need to make sure it helps the company achieve its Purpose. Remember, you ultimately exist to serve the company."

Everyone nodded, and I turned the floor back over to Megan.

"Thanks for that, Will," she said. "Okay, everyone, let's see. It's

Monday . . . how about we let Will go and then spend an hour on the 'why and what' exercise, then plan to regroup on Wednesday to share our three draft statements?"

More nods. Megan looked at me and said, "Want to regroup on Thursday for a call so I can share where we landed?"

"Perfect, and thanks for taking the time, everyone," I said as I grabbed my notebook and headed for the door.

Megan started to get up to walk me out, but I said, "No worries, I know the way. You all stay and get to work. Good luck, team!"

I made my way through their office, deftly sidestepping Rosey, and walked out the door and into the sunlight. As I waited for my Lyft to arrive, I saw a billboard for a pro tennis tournament that was taking place in town.

Most of my middle and high school and college years were spent on the tennis court. I'd learned a lot about teamwork during those years, especially from my college coach, who worked hard to make sure we were functioning well as a unit. He always created opportunities for us to bond, and always reiterated the goal we were chasing. The style was different from how most tennis coaches led, probably because tennis is mostly an individual sport. But I was sure that the team-focused coaching we got was more powerful and ultimately more effective.

In my senior year of college, the team entered the conference tournament ranked eighth. We got matched against the top-ranked team in the first round. Comparing our rosters, you could see that each of their players was more talented than ours.

We should have lost all seven points against them. But that's not what happened.

We focused on supporting players who, on paper, were severely overmatched by their opponent. Anyone on my team who wasn't playing cheered on the teammates who were still competing. The whole tournament came to a head in the third set.

Our number two player, who was from Germany, realized his opponent was also German—and ranked top in the country. He emphatically told us there was absolutely no way he could beat this player. Sure enough, he lost the first set six to one. But inch by inch, shot by shot, he climbed back and won the second set in a tie-breaker. We were tied three to three, and it all came down to our number two versus their number one.

Our team was hooting and hollering with every point our teammate won, shouting encouragement with every point lost, and urging him on. As my teammate won the final point, he clinched *our* victory in the biggest upset in our conference's history.

It was the most exciting moment of my tennis career—and a feeling of "team" that I'd been searching for ever since.

My agency's early days felt very much like those times with the tennis team. When we were less than ten people, the company was extremely close-knit. I never felt like we were out of sync. We celebrated wins with gusto and supported one another when we failed.

But as the company grew, I found it harder and harder to keep that team atmosphere. Sure, our top value was "Team First"—

and I felt like we did a better job than most in living up to that promise—but I still felt something was missing.

And then I thought about Megan's team at SalesLive.

It was clear that each person in that group was a high performer. They were attentive and thoughtful in their comments, and I could see why Shera had thought this team would succeed.

But this team didn't have time to come together in the same way my tennis team had—over years of working together to face challenges and achieve victories. They had to move quickly, and I was hopeful (though yet not entirely confident) that PVTV alone could do it.

The rest of the week was fairly typical. Each morning I would arrive at the office and knock my email inbox down to zero (a habit I had long ago adopted) before moving onto my daily tasks. Usually, as the day progresses, my calendar frees up, allowing me the flexibility to jump on anything urgent. With Rachel running the agency now, my afternoons had more often been dedicated to writing and working on specific initiatives.

On Thursday, I spent most of the day at the office, checking in with Rachel and working on a few writing opportunities. We have a nook in the office that looks out over Foothills Park. It was one of my favorite places for some get-work-done time.

After a few hours of work, stopping only around 11:00 a.m. to grab my daily routine cup of decaf coffee, my phone buzzed. It was Megan, right on time for our 3:00 p.m. update.

"Hey, Megan," I said as I answered the phone.

"Hey, Will. Is this still a good time to chat?"

"You bet. I can't wait to hear how the week has gone!" I said.

"It has gone much better than even I expected. We started off with the first exercise, going over the 'whys' and 'whats' as you suggested."

"And how did that go? Did you have any good dialogue during that part?" I asked.

"Oh, you bet. That's where the most debate came from, actually. But it was," Megan paused, thinking of the right description. "It was different, I guess, than previous debates. Everyone was supportive and actually listened to what the others were saying. Sure enough, we got to a pretty good place after a few hours, and everyone set off to work on their three possible Purpose statements."

She was quiet for a second, and I could hear her shuffling some papers around.

Continuing, she said, "I would say that, for the most part, all of our Purpose statements were in the same ballpark. With a few word changes here and there, we were all landing in the same place."

"Wow! Well, I'm dying to hear where you landed!" I said.

"Before I share it, I need to make sure the direction we headed was appropriate. A big debate we had was whether our Purpose and Vision should focus on us as a team or if it should focus on the product we are creating. Do you have an initial reaction to that?"

"I've seen it done both ways, actually. The goal is for it to be a rallying point and foundational lens for your team, and that can happen if it's focused on the product or the team," I said.

"Great, because we decided to have our Purpose focus on the product. As you know, SalesLive focuses on eliminating the tension between salespeople and their customers. Our product offering will enhance SalesLive's suite of products, and it is meant to help the salesperson form a deeper, more personal bond with the customer."

Megan paused and took a deep breath. I could tell she was a little nervous.

"Okay, here it is. 'Our Purpose is to *strengthen* the relationship between salespeople and their clients,'" she said, emphasizing the word "strengthen."

"Ah, I see. So, while SalesLive overall is working to eliminate tension between salespeople and their clients, your team is creating a product that specifically strengthens the relationship between those two parties, which ultimately will eliminate tension," I said.

"Exactly! Do you think that works?" she asked.

"I believe it does! And everyone on the team agrees?" I asked.

"Yes, everyone is on board. We spent time stress testing it against the company's overall Purpose, making sure that it aligns and supports the current company Purpose, and that it works better for our team than the company's Purpose. We think it satisfies both of those requirements."

"What's been most amazing, though," she said, "is that even though we are just starting this process, and I know we have to even lock in our Purpose before it can have an impact, watching them work together to come up with it is the first time I've actually felt like they were a team."

"That's so great to hear and not surprising. One thing that's happening is that the team knows what they're working on and why. Not knowing the answer to those fundamental questions is one of the main reasons you've seen them struggle. This kind of recognition always brings people together. But I expect the real reason they're enjoying the process is that they're starting to build something together. Something new that they're all a part of, and that's special. I bet *you're* even starting to feel that," I said.

"You know I am!" she said.

We talked for a few more minutes about the session that would take place on Monday morning, where we'd focus on the Vision for the team. It sounded like her team was already starting to noodle on ideas.

VISION

Megan was waiting for me as I entered the SalesLive office. Luckily, Rosey was busy with someone else, so we skirted past her and into the main area. We made chit-chat while making our way to the conference room. (She had a scare with her cat but eventually found her in a small tree in her yard. I lost five rounds of Chutes and Ladders to Danielle.)

"Isn't that game supposed to be random?" she asked as we entered the room.

"Yeah, she had to be cheating. I just haven't figured out how yet," I said.

The team had assembled in the conference room. I took my place at the head of the table.

"Good morning, gang. I hope you all had a terrific weekend!" I said.

Head nods and a few "yeps" followed, and I asked Megan to recap where we were to date.

"Okay, after we met with you last week, we went through the exercises you prescribed and created our team Purpose, which is to strengthen the relationship between a salesperson and their client," she said.

"Great. Could someone else tell me why you chose that statement over the company's Purpose?" I asked.

Hala said, "We debated that and decided that, while our

Purpose statement supports the overall company's Purpose, we needed something more specific to why we exist. The product we are creating focuses entirely on the relationship between the salesperson and their customer, which is only a part of the overall suite of products the company offers."

"Love it. Okay, we're now on to the Vision part of the process. Megan, what is a company or team's Vision?" I asked.

Megan said, "The Vision is the team or company you want to become."

"Exactly. It's a more tangible concept than your Purpose, and it usually is something that should be revisited every three to five years, depending on how relevant it remains. A Vision can change, but Purpose, if done properly, should be evergreen," I said.

I wrote on the whiteboard:

SalesLive Purpose

To eliminate the tension between salespeople and their prospects

SEAL Team X Purpose

To strengthen the relationship between salespeople and their clients

SalesLive Vision

To be the ultimate tool for our customers to achieve their sales goals

SEAL Team X Vision

"As a reminder," I said, "the SalesLive Vision is to be the ultimate tool for our customers to achieve their sales goals. It must be something that we can track in several ways and is a Vision that, if achieved, helps move the company closer toward its Purpose.

"What we want to work on today is finding your team's Vision. The big question we want to answer is, what kind of team do you want to become?"

"Can you give us another example?" asked Dustin, "Maybe tell us what your company's Vision is?"

"Sure, as you know my company is an advertising agency. Our Vision is to be sought after by the world's best companies for our creative problem-solving. That's the company we strive to be. We want to be known for the great work we do and for the best companies in the world to seek us out for it. And we get to decide what 'best' means," I said.

"Has it ever changed?" asked Q.

"It sure has. When we first started, the idea of what we wanted our company to be was a bit different. During annual planning a few years ago, we realized we were on a new path. We revisited our Vision, and sure enough, it was time for a change. But it's important to note that our Purpose has never changed," I said.

"How do you recommend we start figuring out our Vision?" asked Megan.

"Glad you asked," I said, and I stood up and wrote on the board:

EXERCISE: Modeling After Other Teams
EXERCISE: Rumor Mill

"The first exercise I want you to go through is to think about other teams and what about them is so inspiring. These could be sports teams, teams within your company, external companies, and anything in between. The teams that you look to for whatever reason. You can look at them for their qualities as a team, or the output they produce, like their product or service. Everyone with me?" I asked.

Ashley asked, "What do you mean that it can be 'the output they produce'?"

I thought for a moment and asked, "What is your favorite restaurant?"

"Easy, Chefs & Sailors," she said.

"Okay, great. Tell me one thing you like about the restaurant overall, and one thing you like about the food," I said.

"Well, the staff is incredibly attentive and knowledgeable. And the food is always unique, and quite honestly, the most delicious I've ever had," Ashley said.

"Great, so those are two things you can appreciate about Chefs & Sailors. Their Vision could be focused on being the most knowledgeable, attentive restaurant in the world, or it could be to provide their guests with the best-tasting food on every visit. When you create your Vision, it can describe the team you want to become or the product you want to be known for."

"Or both, I suppose," said Dustin. "The Vision for your agency seems to accomplish both."

"I suppose you're right, Dustin," I said. "Good call."

Continuing, I said, "Once you finish the first exercise, the second thing I want you to do is to pretend you're another SalesLive team. You're at the proverbial water cooler, talking about how great SEAL Team X is. What compliments are they sharing about you or your product? What would you want Shera to say? Write down the words that keep bubbling up, as they will help you see what kind of words to use in your Vision statement."

At this point, they were all taking notes, and I could tell they were getting it.

"Now, as you finish with these exercises, I want you to do the same thing you did with your Purpose statement. Everyone should identify three possible Vision statements. You want the sentences you propose to be simple, specific, ambitious, and measurable."

"We should make sure our Vision statement doesn't conflict with SalesLive's Vision statement," said Sasha.

"And," added Hala, "we should make sure that our Vision would help us get closer to achieving our Purpose, right?"

"That's right! I think you guys are getting it," I said, truly proud of them.

After answering a few more questions, I packed up my stuff and, once again, told Megan I would let myself out. This time as I made my way through the lobby, Rosey turned as if sensing me and watched me from the corner of her robotic eyes as I passed, with a slight shake of her head side to side. What was with that robot?

o‑‑o

"This is so frustrating!" Rachel said, a little too loud for our open office environment. Luckily, barely anyone was around.

Tilting my head to the right so I could see her around her monitor, I said (quietly so she would get the hint), "What's wrong?"

"Oh, sorry," she said in almost a whisper. "I'm just really frustrated with Steve's team right now."

"Wait, I thought you were dealing with problems with the creative team?" I asked, because Steve was on our account team.

"I am! Come to think of it, the technology team is also driving me nuts," she said. Scratching her head, she added, "You know, it's hard to find a team that I'm not frustrated with right now."

I looked at my calendar and saw that I had a free hour.

"Rach, got time for a walk-and-talk? We probably have time to hit our favorite spot in the park," I said.

"Yeah, I'm sure some fresh air could do me some good."

A few minutes later, we crossed the street to the park. Over the years, Rachel and I had gravitated toward a spot on the north end where a small stream entered the park. There's a bench just off the path where we'd spent many hours batting around ideas and trying to solve problems.

As we headed toward our spot, I asked her, "So, step back and think about all the problems that are happening with the various teams and team members. Are there any consistencies or themes?"

It was the same question I had asked Matt about his problems at Titan, and I had a feeling I would get a similar answer.

"Will, that's what I've been trying to figure out. It can't be totally coincidental that I'm having so many culture problems right now. We've never had these kinds of issues, at least not on this scale."

Rachel paused thoughtfully. "The best I can figure," she said, "is that people don't seem to feel like they're part of the same team. It's like 'team against team' these days. Creative is mad at accounts, technology is upset with creative, and the account team has just about had it with both of them. It's like each team thinks they're on an island, disconnected from the rest of the company."

I stayed silent, because I've learned over time that letting someone process their thoughts and get it all out is often the best way for them to solve their problems. Usually, they already have the answer. They just need to give it space to come out. I think I learned that from Charles, since he used it on me quite frequently.

"And you know what else? On an individual basis, I see more discontent than ever before. It's like people don't realize how they impact the business! They believe in our Purpose of inspiring happiness, but they don't see how they contribute. The further down the org chart, the more people feel like they don't make a real difference," she said.

Rachel's observations were shocking. We'd always had a great culture. I asked her to give me some examples of how people were acting.

"Just the other day, I was sitting in the account team meeting that Steve was leading. After they went over the numbers, someone said, 'I just don't understand where all the money goes.' Steve asked what he meant, and he said that he saw us doing so well, but he didn't understand how the increase in revenue helped them. He actually said, 'Are we just working to make a bunch of board members rich?' I nearly fell out of my chair when he said that."

"Yikes, that's not good. Now that I think about it, though, I don't know how anyone would know what we do with our profit. Obviously, you and I know where it goes. We need the money to create a cash reserve for down periods, pay off debt, donate to nonprofits, make office upgrades . . . so many things. But how would any team member know that?" Something else occurred to me. "Have we seen a decrease in employee retention?"

"Yes. We are starting to see retention issues. That's new for us, too. It's putting a bigger burden on our recruitment team. As you know, when people leave, it's disruptive on many levels," she said.

We had reached our spot. Luckily, no one was sitting on the bench. We made our way there and sat down. The stream was in good form, full from the previous night's rain. I always loved sitting by a stream or river, taking in the never-ending sound of rushing water.

"I'm really sorry that you're having to deal with this," I said.

"Will, be honest with me. Am I doing something wrong? If I'm failing in any way, you have to tell me. It was a great honor when you handed the company reins over to me, but maybe I'm not ready. I can handle it if that's the case," she said.

"Rachel, you're doing a better job running this company than I ever did! And I'm not just saying that. Our work has never been better, we're winning more than we ever have, and our numbers are up in almost every category! No, this definitely isn't because of you. If anything, things would be worse if not for you."

"Thank you," she said, and I could tell she was a bit embarrassed by the praise. I hoped she believed it because it was all true. I was incredibly proud and impressed by her growth as a leader, and she was doing a better job than I'd done. She was a natural leader.

"I have to believe this has something to do with our growth. I've never run a company this big, either!" I said. The agency had recently hit the 250-person mark.

"Ok, I'll trust you. And thank you. So, I do have an idea," she said.

"Hit me with it."

"Well, you remember when I talked to you about *The Great Game of Business*?" she asked.

"Talked about and then some. Thanks for leaving a copy of the book on my desk. I haven't dived into it yet, but it looks interesting. That's the guy you saw give the keynote speech, correct?"

"That's right, Jack Stack. I think the problems he writes about solving with his Great Game system sound exactly like what we're dealing with. I really think it's something we should consider," she said.

I asked, "Ok, I'll take a look at the book. If we did decide to give it a try, what do you think the next step would be?"

She gave me a big smile and said, "That depends on what you're doing next Tuesday."

Thursday morning, I was up early again to sneak down to the kitchen to talk with Charles. I made coffee and initiated the video chat. This time, I remembered to put my headphones on so I wouldn't wake the family.

Charles came on the screen. I was glad to see him. "Good morning, Charles!"

"It's actually just after noon here, Will, but good morning to you. We arrived here in this rural section of County Clare called Mount Shannon. It's the most amazing little town, right on the western shore of a beautiful freshwater lake called Lough Derg. Hold on, let me show you," he said.

He flipped the camera setting, so it was now focused outward, and I could see the lake.

"What's that in the center of the lake?" I asked.

"Oh, that's the best bit," he said. "They call it St. Patrick's Purgatory. It dates back to the fifth century. It's been undisturbed for over 1,500 years! Apparently, it has been a place of Christian pilgrimage and prayer. It's got an incredible history. We plan to visit this afternoon."

He continued to pan, showing me the most beautiful landscape I had ever seen. It had the deepest green grass, with rolling hills and small mountains in the background.

Charles flipped the camera back to him, saying, "You should consider bringing Sarah and Dani here one day. I can't think of a more peaceful place on Earth."

"I think that sounds like an incredible plan. Where are you headed after this?" I asked.

"We're headed south to Dublin! It should take us about two days. Anyway, Will, catch me up on things. The last time we talked, you were thinking about how to measure PVTV, right?" he asked.

"Right, or at least I was realizing that I had never found a way to measure it. And some of the things you said on that call that can occur when you neglect to measure goals have started to show up in my company and at Matt's," I said.

Charles nodded his head and asked, "And have you come up with any ideas on how to solve these problems?"

"Well, Rachel has brought to my attention something called *The Great Game of Business*. Have you heard of it?"

"I have heard of it. I came across a company that was running it and raved about it. I was well past running companies of my own by then, so I didn't dive too deeply, but I remember how impressed they were," he said.

"Do you remember any of the characteristics of that company? Rachel thinks we need to give it a shot, but I'm not sure," I said.

"Let me think for a second," he said. He was walking around a little outside of the house they were at, and I saw more stunning scenes behind him. I caught sight of an old stone tower and a small bridge over a stream, guessing that they were four or five hundred years old.

He eventually found a spot to sit down, and I saw what looked to be an Irish Setter come up to him.

"The owner gave me a tour of his facility. As I recall, people were exceptionally engaging. He mentioned a number; maybe he called it the 'critical number'? I can't remember exactly, but everyone we met on the tour knew the number and knew how close they were to hitting it. And they seemed to be excited about the work they were doing, which was unique given that many of them were far down the line of production," I said.

"That does sound interesting. Rachel has roped me into going up to their headquarters next week to talk to the CEO of the company and see it in action, so I guess I'll know more then," I said.

"I'll be interested in hearing about that! I have to go in a minute. We'll be spending the night here and then leaving in the morning."

We talked a little more. He told me about seeing an extraordinary creature called the Highland Cow while cycling through Scotland. I told him that Danielle finally scored her first soccer goal. (I didn't mention it was on the wrong side.) We agreed to talk again in the next week or two, but we needed to wait until they settled on the next leg of their trip.

I signed off, and after looking up the Highland Cow, I started doing a little research on The Great Game. I was still skeptical but was becoming more intrigued after hearing Charles's experience. Maybe Rachel was on to something.

TENETS

It was Monday morning, and I was at the SalesLive office again. Rosey seemed to have been replaced by a human, which was a relief.

I checked in with little hassle and sat down to wait for Megan. Earlier in the week, she had updated me on how the team had fared with the Vision statement exercise.

"This was a wild one," she said. "We were all over the place as we went through the two exercises. We started with talking about teams that we wanted to emulate. That led to a big debate about which was the better team, the Patriots or the Cowboys. Eventually, we coalesced around a handful of teams or companies we could agree epitomized excellence—Apple, Tesla, the founding team of SalesLive, and yes, the Patriots," she said.

"I remember that early SalesLive team," I said. "You're not wrong there. So what characteristics did all of those teams have?"

"We found a lot of common attributes," she said. I could hear her flipping through some notes. "They all worked seamlessly as a team toward a common goal, and they were able to create a competitive advantage that was extremely hard to beat."

"Love it. And what about the second exercise? I think I called it the 'Rumor Mill'," I asked.

"That one was easier. We went around and asked what we'd want people saying about us, and there was one overriding theme that rose to the surface. We all wanted to hear that our product was the favorite of the salespeople. We imagined other teams admiring our product and telling us that their customers couldn't live without it. We hoped these other teams would wonder how they could make their product that indispensable," she said.

We had talked more about the process, too. I thought the team's Vision statement was terrific. She had also shared once again how much better the team was already working together. I was really optimistic about this session.

"Hey, Will!" Megan said, entering the lobby.

"Good morning! Hey, what happened to your robot?" I asked as we made our way into the main area.

"Huh, I don't know. I think sometimes maybe Rosey takes a break to get a software update or something. How come?" she asked.

"Oh, no reason." I wasn't going to admit it, but I had prepared an entirely new approach to try to win her favor. I was a bit disappointed not to get the chance to use it.

We entered the conference room, and the group seemed more engaged with each other than I'd previously seen. They were going back and forth about some TV show that some of them loved and some hated. There was some good-natured kidding. All in all, they seemed much more relaxed and comfortable with each other than I remembered.

"Hey, everyone, ready to get started?" I asked.

After a round of yes's (with a solid "Jawohl!" from Sasha), I asked Megan to recap and set up the day.

"Okay, team. We're on a path to create our PVTV, ensuring it's in alignment with SalesLive's overall PVTV. So far, we have created our Purpose and Vision, and today we will work on our Tenets," she said. "Does anyone remember what our Tenets are?"

When we started the process, Megan told me that she required the entire team to read my book, *The 5-Day Turnaround*, to be as prepared as possible for this process. She had re-read it, she had proudly informed me.

Q said, "I got this one. The Tenets are the things we will do to accomplish our Vision."

"Perfect! Well, at least I think it is," she said, giggling a little. "Will, that's correct, right?"

Laughing, I said, "Absolutely. Who wants to repeat your team's Purpose by heart?"

Several hands raised, and I called on Hala. She said, "Our Purpose is to strengthen the relationship between salespeople and their clients."

"Is that correct?" I asked, looking around the room. Head nods all around. "Okay, who wants to repeat your team's Vision by heart?"

Megan was the only one that raised her hand. I wasn't surprised. Memorizing wasn't easy, and Megan was the Everest of over-achievers. I nodded for her to go ahead.

"Our Vision is to be the most indispensable tool in the salesperson's toolbox."

I stood up and, looking at my notes, wrote on the whiteboard:

SalesLive Purpose

To eliminate the tension between salespeople and their prospects

Seal Team X Purpose

To strengthen the relationship between salespeople and their clients

SalesLive Vision

To be the ultimate tool for our customers to achieve their sales goals

Seal Team X Vision

To be the most indispensable tool in the salesperson's toolbox

"Before we jump into our Tenets, do you see how your Purpose and Vision help the company have a better chance at accomplishing its Purpose and Vision?"

Dustin chimed in. "Yes. For example, when we think about our Purpose as we strengthen the relationship between salespeople and clients, we will be eliminating the tension between them."

"And the same applies to our Vision," Ashley added. "If we become the most indispensable tool in our customer's toolbox, we'll be helping SalesLive overall become the ultimate tool for our customers."

"Bingo!" I said. "You guys are getting it. Okay, let's talk about Tenets. As Q pointed out, our Tenets are the things we need to do to achieve our Vision."

"I always recommend having three core Tenets if you can. We want people to be able to remember them. They should be concise and actionable."

"What are your company's Tenets again?" asked Sasha.

"Great question, Sasha," I said. "I'll start with our Vision so that the Tenets make sense. Our Vision is to be sought after by the world's best companies for our creative problem-solving. And then we always express our Tenets in this way. We will do this by attracting and retaining exceptional people, building remarkable products and experiences, and striving for operational excellence." They were all furiously writing notes, so I added, "Think of it like this. We want the best companies in the world to seek us out. We believe that if we have amazing people, and if we build amazing products, and if we run our company effectively, then we'll achieve that Vision."

"That makes a lot of sense, especially since you're in the advertising industry," said Hala. "How do you suggest we go about creating our Vision?"

Sasha spoke up. "Let me guess; you have two exercises for us to work through."

I smiled at the team. "You know it."

I wrote on the whiteboard.

EXERCISE: The Kitchen Sink
EXERCISE: Why We Failed

"For the first exercise, I want you to fill this whiteboard with every possible thing you can think of that your team will need to do to achieve your Vision. Every idea is a good one. Choose one person to write on the board, and the rest of you throw as many ideas up as possible," I said. "Ashley, name one thing your team will have to do to achieve its Vision."

She thought for a moment and then said, "If we wanted to be the most indispensable tool for salespeople, I assume we'd need it to be extremely stable. If our product crashed a lot, they'd never value it enough."

"And we'd need to have a great user experience. The product would need to be intuitive and meet the customer's needs as fast as possible," added Dustin.

"Great, you both nailed it. All of that should go on the board. After you finish with that, I want you all to independently write down five reasons why you might fail to achieve your Vision. Focus on things in your control as a team."

More note-taking, and then Megan said, "Got it. And then I'm guessing we follow the same process as before. We come together and share our reasons, having a healthy debate about each of these exercises."

"You're getting good at this, Megan," I said, smiling. "That's exactly right. After that, you'll start trying to find three buckets

91

that encapsulate all of that brainstorming. There should be several themes that rise to the top. When you finally write the statements, you should be able to place each item under at least one of them."

I could tell the team was ready for me to leave the room so they could get to work. Megan and I agreed to connect later in the week, and I took my leave, proud of the team. It was great to see how quickly they were embracing the PVTV concept. It helped that they understood the model because of SalesLive, but I thought it was more likely a result of their need to feel like they were part of a team.

"Buckle up, boss. We're about to take off."

I buckled myself into my seat on the plane and said, "Rachel, are you sure this trip is necessary? Couldn't we just set up a call with Jack or someone on his team to learn more about The Great Game?"

Before she could answer, the pilot came on over the loudspeaker and talked about our flight to Springfield, Missouri.

When he finished, Rachel said, "It's a little late for that now. Besides, I think we need to experience The Great Game for ourselves. From what I've read, nothing beats going straight to the source."

During the flight, Rachel gave me more background on Jack Stack's company, Springfield Remanufacturing Corp, or SRC. SRC was established in 1983 when 13 employees purchased a part of

International Harvester, a company that rebuilt truck engines. The employees invested $100,000 of their own money and $8.9 million in loans to save 119 jobs. By 1988, SRC had a value of $43 million.

"Can you believe that? In just five years, the company went from being on the brink of closing down to be worth $43 million! And now, I've heard company sales have reached close to $1 billion with all of the joint ventures and new services they've created. It's quite a turnaround story. Hey! That's the kind of story that could have fit right in your book!" she said.

I couldn't disagree with her. She shared more about SRC as the flight continued. It truly was impressive what Jack and the team had done. "Do you think we'll get to meet Jack while we're there?" I asked.

"They said it was a possibility, but no guarantees. While I hear that Jack spends quite a bit of time at The Great Game office, he is also running SRC, which takes up most of his time," she said.

We landed at the Springfield-Branson National Airport. The moment we departed the plane, we noticed Springfield's pride in its business community. There were promotional signs on the corridor walls for various local companies. I got the sense that many people who traveled through this airport were business travelers—or bass fishermen. If the many bass fishing signs didn't give away that detail, the impressively large bass replica in the middle of the lobby did.

We grabbed a Lyft and headed for The Great Game office. I was immediately struck by how flat the landscape was. You could see for miles. After a few minutes, I caught sight of a large SRC sign in front of a building.

"Is that where we're headed?" I asked the Lyft driver, pointing at the building.

"No, that's the original Springfield Remanufacturing factory. I'm taking you to one of the new locations," he said.

"So you're familiar with the company, then?" Rachel asked.

"Oh, sure, everybody is around here. They've been great, creating hundreds of jobs over the years and giving back to the community in so many ways," he said. "My brother-in-law has worked at one of the factories for over 20 years!" He was clearly proud of this connection to the company.

Rachel had shared the exceptional employee retention that SRC had achieved after creating The Great Game of Business. I was getting excited to see this thing in action.

"This is Sunshine Street," the driver said. "There are a lot of great restaurants and places to shop if you're in town long enough. And here we are, SRC Electrical and The Great Game. They're both in that big building there."

He pulled up to an industrial-looking building that I could tell was built in the 1970s or 80s. We jumped out and saw that there was a specific lobby for The Great Game. We checked in with the receptionist and took a seat in a strikingly modest waiting area.

I nudged Rachel and said, "Given how successful they've been, I'm surprised they haven't upgraded their office."

"I'm pretty sure that's due to The Great Game. From what I've read, they spend extra profit on their employees, not a glitzy office," she said.

As people passed by, I noticed how casual they all were. When the big door at the end of the hall in front of us opened, I could tell there was a factory. As people entered and exited, they were all wearing safety goggles and protective gear, almost all were in jeans, and many wore hats.

And they all looked happy. We saw smiles and high-fives everywhere.

A woman came up to us and, extending her hand to Rachel, said, "Hello, you must be Rachel! I'm Linda. We're so glad you could come for a visit!"

Rachel and I stood up, and Rachel said, "We couldn't be more appreciative of your time. This is my partner, Will."

I shook Linda's hand and asked, "Thanks so much for having us. So, what do you have in store for us?"

Linda said, "From what you told me, Rachel, your company is considering running The Great Game. Well, we just love to share what's involved and give a first-person view of The Game in action! I thought what we'd do first is . . ."

Just then, we heard a voice behind us. We turned to see a man coming toward us, saying, "Linda, what do we have here?"

He was wearing a gray suit jacket and dark slacks and had neat, slightly graying hair. I saw a big smile come across Rachel's face.

"Well, Jack, this is Rachel and Will. They're here to learn more about The Great Game," she said.

"Is that right? And how did you hear about us?" he asked, shaking our hands.

"I saw you speak at a conference about a month ago. You gave the closing keynote address. I was hooked and have been thinking about The Great Game since," Rachel said.

"Oh, of course. I remember that. I try to do things like that as little as possible, honestly. But I guess it went well enough if you ended up here," Jack said graciously.

I was trying to place his accent. He sounded like my relatives in Chicago, but he spoke with a bit more of a drawl than they did. I liked him immediately.

"How long are you in town for?" he asked.

Rachel said, "We were planning on spending a few hours here, and then Linda set us up to meet with a company nearby that also runs The Great Game, and then we head back later in the afternoon."

"Well, if they're only here with us for a few hours, then I better take it from here, Linda. They need to see behind the curtain. I think I'll take them over to Heavy Duty," he said.

Linda gave us a bit of a shrug and a big grin, "You're in Jack's hands now. Good luck to you both!" She turned to Jack. "Will and Rachel have an appointment with Little Solutions at 2:00

p.m. The office is about 10 minutes away from here, so just make sure you leave on time."

"Don't worry, I'll make sure they get to Molly's shop on time. Let's go, folks."

We followed Jack outside to his truck. It was a four-door black GM pickup truck and looked as if someone had recently washed it. I jumped in the back while Rachel joined Jack in the front. When he turned on the car, talk radio came on.

Turning down the radio, Jack said, "Sorry about that. I try to maximize every part of the day, and listening to business talk shows while I drive is one way I keep up with the markets."

"Where are we headed?" I asked.

"I'm taking you to where it all began! Our Heavy Duty factory, as we call it, is closer to the airport. That's the best place to get a real sense of The Game," he said.

"We can't thank you enough for taking this time with us, Jack," Rachel said. "I can't help but think you have much better things to do. The Great Game must be really important to you."

"Well, I can't think of anything better than exposing new people to what we're doing at SRC and to The Great Game. It's become the most important aspect of our entire business. I don't know where we'd be without it. And the idea of helping others find that kind of success with their business is a real passion for me."

I said, "I'm curious, Jack, it seems like such a great platform to run a business. I can't imagine any leader that learns about your program wouldn't immediately sign up!"

"Many do, but you'd be surprised how often leaders get scared by the open-book management component. As you probably know, to play The Game, your business is required to open up its books to the team. The idea of the team seeing the financials is just too scary for most leaders." He added, chuckling, "Personally, I think the idea of your company going out of business is much scarier than your team members seeing a Profit & Loss Statement, but what do I know."

We nodded, listening and thinking about how valid his observations were.

Jack continued, "Also, I don't like to think of it as open-book management. That concept has been around a long time, and the issue isn't as much about the open-book part. It's that nobody wants to be *managed*. People want to be led! I much prefer the term open-book *leadership*."

We pulled into the parking lot of a building.

"This is where it all started," Jack said as he parked the car. "The original business was combine and truck engines, and as we grew, we named this factory, 'Heavy Duty'."

We followed him into the building and once again found a very modest, simple lobby. He had us check in with the receptionist, who gave each of us a name badge and a pair of safety goggles.

After chit-chatting with the receptionist (Jack seemed to know everyone), he said, "All right, let's get started. See this yellow line on the floor? We're going to follow that as much as possible through the factory floor."

He led us to two big swinging doors at the end of the hallway, and when he opened them, the room's massiveness took me aback. It must have been close to 40,000 square feet, with a flat roof and wide-open expanse. Everything appeared to be right angles and very organized. Throughout the room, you could see sparks flying, conveyor belts humming, people gathered together working, and an overall sense of energy and activity.

And the sounds flowing through the room were just what you'd expect from such a setting. The beeping noises of a forklift backing up, metal clanks, and the sound of grinders and other mechanical gear being used to its fullest filled the air. I was overwhelmed by the desire to grab a wrench and get to work!

Almost as soon as we entered, a large man in overalls and a camouflage hunting hat came up to Jack and said, "How'd you do in the tournament last weekend?"

They shook hands, and Jack introduced us to his friend Larry before turning back to him. "Not as good as I would have with you on the team, I'll tell you that. I didn't win, which is all that matters."

"You'll get 'em next time, boss," he said and excused himself.

Rachel asked, "So what kind of tournament were you in?"

"Bass fishing. You two do a lot of fishing?" he asked.

We both said no, and Jack said, "I know what you're thinking. Who has time to sit in a boat for five hours just watching the time tick by? But that's now how I do it. If I'm going to fish or bowl, or golf, I want it to be a competition. That way, there's something at stake! It always brings out the best in me when I know there is something on the line.

"Speaking of there being something on the line," he said as we approached a woman sitting on a forklift looking at a clipboard. "Hey, Margory, would you let our guests know what's at stake for your bonus if you hit your target this year?"

"Oh, hey, Jack, didn't see you there," Margory said as she looked down at us. "And, hi, friends of Jack! Happy to share. I'm up for a $6,323 bonus if we hit our numbers this year!"

"And how are you doing so far?" Jack asked.

"Well, our Critical Number this year is focused on free cash flow. At last week's Huddle, we saw that we were just below our threshold for The Critical Number, which basically means our cash flow was lower than it should be. So we decided to focus the past week on inventory turnover because we saw it was getting a little low. In fact, we created MiniGame to focus on that detail," she said. Looking at her watch, she added, "We have our Huddle in a few minutes if you want to see all these details in action."

"Perfect! I was just taking them back to the breakroom. We'll head there now," Jack said.

As we followed the yellow tape toward the breakroom, people would high-five or wave to Jack. He obviously was someone they all liked and admired. There was a broad mix of young and older workers. The more senior team members were more casual with Jack, while the younger ones seemed to be a little in awe of their accomplished leader.

We followed Jack into the breakroom. It was a large area that, like everything else, was meticulously clean.

"Looks like we're a few minutes early. What else can I tell you about The Great Game?" he asked.

Rachel said, "So if I recall correctly, the major elements of The Great Game are The Critical Number, the weekly Huddle, and the bonus that's tied to hitting The Critical Number. Is that right?"

Jack said, "Close, but not exactly. Here's the best way to think about The Great Game of Business."

He walked up to the whiteboard and grabbed a marker. He drew three overlapping circles. In the one on the top left, he wrote, "Know & Teach the Rules." In the one on the top right, he wrote, "Follow the Action & Keep Score." In the circle on the bottom, he wrote, "Provide a Stake in the Outcome."

"These are the three core areas of The Great Game. And right here in the middle, you have The Critical Number."

He then wrote "Critical Number" in the center where the three circles came together.

"You start with knowing and teaching the rules. It's important that everyone knows The Game you're playing. Just like a sports team, imagine if the players didn't know all the rules. For our teams, this includes a lot of financial education. And a key is to continue educating them about the business and how to play The Game," he said.

"Then you want to create a way for everyone to follow the progress. A critical way this happens is with the weekly Huddle. That's what we're about to experience in a few minutes. And then, of course, everyone has to have a stake in the outcome! We do this through a bonus system that pays out each quarter and usually rolls forward throughout the year in case the team doesn't hit the quarterly goal," he said.

"That's something I really love about the model. It always gives people a chance to work hard and hit the goal at the end of the year," Rachel said.

"Exactly. I love knowing people always have a chance to win, especially because it often comes down to that last quarter to get on track to win in the end," he said.

"And what exactly is The Critical Number meant to be for an organization?" I asked.

"Above everything else, The Critical Number defines winning," Jack said. "It gives the team a chance to rally together around a common goal and focus on the most important thing for the company that year. As you heard from Margory, their business is focusing on free cash flow. Think about that for a minute. Here's someone who's running a forklift, and her number one goal is how she can help the company manage its cash flow better. Tell me another place where that happens!"

I couldn't think of another company where the employees down the line knew that kind of financial data, much less how they could impact it.

"The key is if you want people to think and act like owners, you have to treat them like owners. You have to bring them together and ask for their input," Jack said.

Just then, people started filing into the room. As more people came in, we moved toward the back wall. I could see a ripple of awareness and excitement work its way through the room as people realized Jack was in attendance.

Everyone was lining up in front of a large whiteboard on the wall. At the top of the board read, "Heavy Duty Great Game." Someone had set up the board as a chart. There was a column for each quarter, and the rows were metrics. We were halfway through the year, so there were actuals in columns one and two and goals listed in columns three and four.

A man who looked to be 6'4" walked to the front and said in a loud baritone voice, "Who's ready for the weekly Huddle?"

Everyone cheered, and he got started. I was struck by how excited everyone was to be a part of the meeting. And they were talking mostly about finances!

They spent time talking about their progress, essentially walking through each of the rows going across the quarter. They included what appeared to be every source of revenue and expenses for their business.

As they finished working through that chart, the leader walked over to a smaller board with "Inventory Threshold MiniGame" written on it.

Once again, I leaned over to Jack and asked, "I'm guessing the teams use MiniGames when they're looking for a fun way to enhance a particular metric or hit a smaller goal?"

"Exactly. MiniGames are an important part of The Great Game and can make the difference between a team hitting their Critical Number or not. And they are a great way to fix issues by playing games that create behavioral changes. Each MiniGame has a scoreboard and reward for winning. You can think of it as a smaller version of The Great Game," he said.

The rest of the meeting, which lasted exactly 30 minutes, was full of questions—and laughter. I couldn't get over how much fun everyone was having with this.

After it was over, Jack introduced us to a few people. We had a good time hearing some of them telling stories about the good ol' days. Then Jack looked at his watch and said, "Okay, you two, I think you need to leave in a minute to head over to Little Solutions. Do I need to take you back to headquarters to get your car?"

"Nope, we're using Lyft, so we can just call one to pick us up here," Rachel said.

"Great, well, let me walk you out."

Making our way through the factory once again, I could see everyone had gone immediately back to work. I got the sense that each person knew that what they were doing was essential to the company overall.

We ended up in the lobby and turned in our safety goggles and badges.

"The next time you come, I'll take you bass fishing. It'll be fun to see who can catch the biggest fish," Jack said, shaking our hands.

While we were waiting for the Lyft, Rachel and I silently reflected on the experience. I'd never seen anything like it, and I wondered if that was because the model needed Jack Stack at the helm to work.

It took about 15 minutes to get to the Little Solutions office. There was nothing little about it. Their building was four floors and appeared to be made entirely of glass.

We entered the lobby, and whereas SRC was industrial and practical, this office was chic and modern. After we checked in and received our badges (no need for safety goggles here), we sat on a couch and began checking our phones for any messages.

"Ugh, looks like another person has quit," Rachel said. "That makes four people this month. I know with a business over 200 people there will be turnover, but this is too much."

"Do you have the exit interview there?" I asked.

"Yeah, though I haven't read it yet. Martha attached it to the email and gave an overview. Essentially, she said the person was looking for something more, whatever that means," she said.

"Hi. Are you Rachel?"

A woman approached us. She was tall, with long brown hair, and dressed as if she was about to be in a photoshoot.

"I'm Molly. Great to meet you," she said as she shook Rachel's hand. She looked at me and said, "Oh, hi! Sorry, I didn't realize there'd be two of you."

We shook hands, and I said, "I'm Will, and basically, I do what Rachel tells me. She probably wasn't sure I'd agree to come on this trip when she set up the meeting."

"Ah, he's a skeptical one then, isn't he?" she asked Rachel.

"He can be, but he's all right," she said, elbowing me playfully.

Molly smiled and led us out of the lobby. "So we're here to talk about The Great Game, right?"

"That's right, and we're particularly interested in hearing how you've made it work for a consulting business. We also run a services model, which is very different from SRC," Rachel said.

"True," Molly said as she opened a conference door for us. We walked in and sat down at a large conference room table. "I struggled with that as well. I'm lucky that Jack is in the area and always open to giving advice on the topic of The Great Game. He helped me think it through."

"What does your business do, exactly?" I asked.

"We are a consulting firm that believes smaller is better. We help companies reduce their business operations while increasing their revenue and profit," Molly answered.

"*Little* Solutions, I get it," I said. "How long have you been in business?"

"We're going on seven years," she said. "And the company recently hit 250 employees."

"Wow, that's just about the same as our business," Rachel said. "And how long have you been running The Great Game?"

She looked up for a moment, thinking, and said, "I think this is our third year. After we hit 100 employees, that's when I realized we needed to be doing something different. Everything just started to feel . . ."

"Different?" Rachel said, jumping in.

"Exactly! Like, where did we lose that 'all in it together' mentality? I couldn't figure out why things were starting to break down. I was sure it had something to do with our growth, and likely because I couldn't work directly with all the team members as I had when we first started. It was right about then that I saw a write-up in the local paper about SRC's success. I knew of SRC, of course. They've done some great things to help this community. But I always thought of them as just a manufacturing company, not an organization that had anything to do with my business.

"In the article, Jack talked about *The Great Game of Business*, and everything started to click. I immediately reached out to him, went on a tour of one of their factories, and then I was hooked. We've been running The Great Game ever since," she said.

"Was it hard setting it up initially, given how different your business is from SRC?" I asked.

"Actually, not at all." Molly paused a moment, then continued, "Well, truthfully, in the beginning, I was pulling my hair out a bit. But then I remembered, I'm a consultant! I can do this! So I broke it down to its most fundamental aspect. I was trying to bring everyone together around a common goal and give them a way to benefit from the company's success. That's when it all started to make sense."

"Now that you're at 250 people, are you doing anything differently with The Great Game?" Rachel asked.

"Good question. We're about to start something new, actually. I've always thought about The Great Game as an overall company model, and it certainly is, but as we've grown, I've started to wonder what it would be like to have individual teams run their own Great Games. The only thing I think we're missing is an overall sense of belief in what we're doing as a company. So I'm working on that as well," she said.

I smiled and said, "I have an idea for you! Let me tell you about this system *we* use called PVTV."

We went back and forth for about 45 minutes, with Molly sharing her Great Game experience and us sharing our PVTV experience. I had a feeling this must have been what it felt like when the peanut butter company first sat down to form a partnership with the jelly company. By the time we left, my head was swimming with ideas, and Rachel and I both had pages and pages of notes.

The trip to visit SRC to learn more about The Great Game of Business was refreshing in ways I hadn't expected. Just seeing the level of engagement that the employees of SRC and Little Solutions showed was so inspiring. And it was clear that they all felt they were part of a dedicated team.

Rachel had indicated that she wanted another week to think about whether or not the system would work for our agency, but I was pretty sure she'd like to give it a try.

My phone buzzed, and I saw that it was Megan. Sure enough, it was 2:00 p.m. on Friday, exactly when we had agreed to connect.

"Hey, Megan," I said.

"Hi, Will! How's your week been?" she asked.

I gave her a quick update on how the SRC trip had gone, and she immediately started quizzing me about The Great Game.

"Tell you what, when I come over on Monday for our Values

workshop, I'll bring you a copy of the book. Rachel bought a few extras at the conference a few weeks back," I said.

"That would be great!"

"But let's focus on implementing PVTV before you start another crusade," I said, laughing.

"You got it. On that note, I'll catch you up on how our work on the Tenets went. First, we quickly filled the entire whiteboard with the 'Kitchen Sink' exercise you gave us. It felt a bit overwhelming, if I'm honest, looking at all the things we'd need to do to achieve our Vision of being the most indispensable tool in the salesperson's toolbox," she said.

"I'm sure it was, but your Vision is lofty, right? That's a good thing, but to be that valuable to your customer, you're going to have to do a lot!"

"True," she said, laughing. "The next exercise, 'Why We Failed,' was a bit more complicated. You're talking about a team of over-achievers, so thinking about why we might fail was tough. But then Hala suggested another exercise that helped us with that."

"Interesting. What did she suggest?" I asked.

"She had us create a fake PR story about why SalesLive was shutting down our product and dismantling the team. That forced us to step outside of ourselves and look at the issue from a top-down perspective. From that viewpoint, we found many things that could go wrong, and by the end of the exercise, we had a solid list of things to make sure *didn't* happen.

"After that, we worked hard to get all of those items into three tidy buckets. That took the longest time, but eventually, we got there! Here is where we landed: Our Vision is to be the most indispensable tool in the salesperson's toolbox. We will do this by maximizing our strengths as a team, always keeping the salesperson in mind, and focusing on quality over quantity."

Writing those down, I said, "I love those. Tell you what, when we meet Monday I want to ask the group more about why those were the correct Tenets. It will be interesting to see how they support them and who is the most excited about each one."

"Sounds like a plan! Anything I need to do to prepare for the Values conversation?" she asked.

"No. Just make sure you're familiar with SalesLive's Values, which I know you are. Have a great weekend," I said.

"You, too!"

As I hung up, I looked down at the Tenets I had written on my notepad. I was curious why they focused more on the team than the product they were building. I'd have to dig into that when I meet with them.

VALUES

The weekend had been relaxing in all the right ways. On Saturday, the weather was brilliant, so Sarah and I took Danielle to a park with several hiking trails and playgrounds. After exploring one of the paths and seeing that Danielle's little legs were getting tired, we decided to stop near a small brook to have our picnic lunch. I set up the blanket, and Sarah handed out the sandwiches—peanut butter and jelly for Danielle, a turkey and cheese hoagie for me, and a cheese and tomato basil panini for herself.

Danielle grabbed her sandwich and walked over to the stream to see if there were any fish. Watching her, I couldn't believe how quickly she was growing up.

"So you had a good time on that trip, didn't you?" Sarah asked.

"The trip to Springfield? I sure did," I said.

She smiled and said, "I guess Rachel knows what she's doing after all."

"Now, now, don't act like you're the one that discovered her brilliance; I'm the one that made her president of the company! But yes, I was skeptical about the trip. As usual, though, her instincts were right on."

Danielle came back and grabbed some grapes, then headed back to the stream.

"How could you tell I enjoyed the trip?" I asked. "We didn't get a chance to talk about it yet."

"Ever since you got back, you've had a new pep in your step. And more than once, I've watched your mind drift off somewhere. I'm guessing you're thinking about something you experienced while you were up there," Sarah said.

"Yeah, I haven't been able to stop thinking about the process they run at the companies we visited. It's called The Great Game of Business, and it's the first way to run a company I've seen that reminds me of my old college tennis days. I think they've cracked the code on making the team feel more like an actual team!"

"Are you and Rachel thinking of trying it at your agency?"

"I'm going to let Rachel make the decision, but I would be shocked if we don't give it a try. Some of the problems she's been telling me about sure do seem like things that would go away if we could successfully implement The Great Game. Even though she was the one that brought it to me, I think I might be more excited about it than her at this point!" I said.

Sarah laughed and said, "That's probably because she's the one who will have to make it happen!"

I laughed as well, knowing there was some real truth to that. Aside from liking the concept, Rachel would have to do the hard work of figuring out how to implement it at our shop. Of course, I would be there to help, but she ran the company day-to-day and would need to bring it to life. That would require many moving pieces. First, she'd have to get the leadership team on board, which would take some time.

I was lost in thought when Danielle snuck up behind me and put her hands over my eyes.

"BOO! Guess who?"

"Let me see," I said and began to feel her hands. "I can't be sure, but these hands feel like . . . yep, I'm sure of it, these hands belong to a scary zombie!"

I reached back and grabbed her, pulling her upside down over my head and tickling her. She got up and tackled me, embracing the zombie theme and pretending to try to eat me. Soon, she turned me into a zombie, and we looked over at Sarah with hunger in our eyes.

"Oh no you don't!" Sarah said and got up off the blanket. We chased Sarah around for a bit, eventually bringing her over to the world of the undead as well.

"Good morning, Will!" Megan said as she entered the lobby.

I had only been waiting for a few minutes, lamenting the fact that Rosey was still absent from her post. I had some excellent zingers I wanted to try out on her to win her affection.

"Good morning!" I said. "Here's *The Great Game of Business* book that I said I'd bring. Sorry in advance for the notes and highlighted bits."

She thumbed through the book as we walked. "I can't wait to read this, thanks! It looks like you really got into this one."

"It's pretty intriguing. I haven't seen anything like it, and I'm surprised I never heard of it before. It's been around for years!"

We entered the conference room. Megan's team was already in their seats, once again bantering back and forth. After chatting for a bit about everyone's weekend activities, I started writing our progress to date on the whiteboard.

SalesLive Purpose

To eliminate the tension between salespeople and their prospects

SEAL Team X Purpose

To strengthen the relationship between salespeople and their clients

SalesLive Vision

To be the ultimate tool for our customers to achieve their sales goals

SEAL Team X Vision

To be the most indispensable tool in the salesperson's toolbox

SalesLive Tenets

We will do this by putting the customer first, believing in each other, and focusing on profitable growth

SEAL Team X Tenets

We will do this by maximizing our strengths as a team, always keeping the salesperson in mind, and focusing on quality over quantity

"So, how do we feel about the Tenets?" I asked.

Q immediately spoke up. "I'm so pumped up about them! And what's interesting is, I took a stab on my own at what I thought our Tenets would be, and they're extremely different from these. But after working through it with the team, I'm 100% confident these are the right ones."

"I love how we each think about how these Tenets work for the team and how we can use them as a guide as we build our product. For me, focusing on quality over quantity will help me as I map out the creative elements," said Dustin.

"And I love that we have the phrase 'always keep the salesperson in mind' because that's literally my job!" said Ashley.

Several others chimed in, and it was clear that they had nailed the Tenets.

"That's great, everyone," I said, cutting in. "And the important thing is that you continuously refer to the Tenets as you go forward. They should be the lens you use to weigh big decisions, map out your short-term strategy, and help solve debates.

"Now it's time to talk about your team's Values, the final piece of the puzzle," I said.

I walked up to the whiteboard and wrote:

SalesLive Values

We believe in being all for one and one for all, gaining advantage, and always being two steps ahead

"I've always liked the company's Values," said Sasha. "Do we have the option of keeping them if they fit our team?"

"Absolutely! The Purpose and Values can be the same for a team within a company. The Vision and Tenets will always be unique. But even if you all like these Values, we need to go through the process to see if they're right for you," I said. "Let's start with what makes good Values."

I turned back to the whiteboard and wrote:

GOOD VALUES ARE:

- *UNIFYING*
- *NON-NEGOTIABLE*
- *SUCCINCT AND CLEAR*
- *ACTIONABLE*

"Ok, I'll explain what the first bullet means, but then I want someone else to take a stab at each of the remaining ones. Values that are unifying bring the team together. Everyone must deeply believe in each Value. Otherwise, they will result in division among the team. Ok, who wants to do 'non-negotiable'?"

Megan said, "I'll take it. Our Values should be required. We should demand that we each live the Values in everything we do, and any new team members should clearly demonstrate the Values before we consider bringing them on."

"What about partners?" asked Q.

Before I could answer, Megan spoke up.

"My guess, and correct me if I'm wrong, Will, is that we should expect that our partners are not in conflict with our Values. I doubt we can require that all of our partners actively follow our Values—how would we?—but I think we could easily decide if a partner was exhibiting behavior that was in contrast to our Values."

"That's exactly right, Megan, and great question, Q," I said. "It's important that the Values guide our behaviors, including deciding what clients we work with. Who wants to tackle 'succinct and clear'?"

Sasha sheepishly said, "That depends on what succinct means?"

He laughed, as did the rest of the team. Sasha's occasionally limited English was a running theme and good-natured source of teasing.

"Sorry about that, Sasha. 'Succinct' means short. Basically, you want the Values to be crisp and clear so that anyone can understand them. That means we should avoid descriptive, flowery language. Our Values should make sense to anyone," I said. "Unlike my exercises, apparently."

Another round of laughter.

"Ok, so I guess I just did that one," I said. "The last one is 'actionable.' Who wants it?"

Hala said, "This one is all me. Our Values should be things we can act on. If we write them so that we can't see clear behavior that would align with them, we have missed the mark. We should be able to look back at our Values and see if our behaviors line up with them."

"That's great, thanks, Hala," I said. "Now it's time for your two Value exercises."

I walked up to the whiteboard and wrote:

EXERCISE: Modeling
—REFINE, THEN—

EXERCISE: Answer The Tough Questions

- *What does the Value mean to me? To us?*
- *What actions can we connect to this Value (within the team, with customers and partners, etc.)?*
- *How could this Value be misinterpreted?*
- *How will we measure this Value?*

"Your first exercise is one of my favorites. You will start on your own, listing people that you want to emulate. Think of the people in your life you respect the most. They could be people in this room, friends or family, or even someone you've never met. Once you have a list of around five people, you'll start thinking about why you listed each person. What traits do they have that you want to have? What behaviors are they showing that you want to do more of?

"Then you will all share those values with the group. Use the whiteboard, and start to group them into categories. What themes bubble up to the top? Ultimately, you want to get to three to five Values. Don't worry about what to call them at this point. We just want the theme or overall feeling.

"Once you have those, you can move on to exercise two. Work through the questions I listed on the board, making sure you can answer each of them for the Values you landed on. Everyone with me so far?"

Head nods across the board again, and lots of note-taking. I continued.

"By the end of that process, you should have a solid list of pressure-tested Values that you can begin shaping into a statement. Use the phrase, "We believe in . . ." and finish the sentence accordingly," I said.

Everyone seemed on board, and once again, eager to get started. I said my good-byes, and Megan and I decided to connect on Friday about their progress.

Out of the corner of my eye, I noticed someone waving at me. I peered around my monitor. Sure enough, Rachel was waving to get my attention. I took out my earbuds, which were blaring an REM playlist. (When I needed to focus and crank out work, I usually opted for the familiar REM songs from my youth.)

"What's up?" I asked.

"So I've been thinking about *The Great Game of Business*. A lot. And I'm ready to move forward. I know you're skeptical because it would be such a big change, but I'm as sure as I can be that it's just what we need. The more I look at the problems we're facing and then compare them to the case studies of companies that have embraced The Great Game, it just becomes more obvious that *this* is what we need!"

I could tell she was ramping up to make her case, so I decided to interject.

"Sounds great!" I said.

"Well, it's just that . . . wait, what?"

"I said, 'it sounds great.' I'm sure you've thought it through, and to be honest, I'm a big fan as well. It's your shop to run now. Just let me know how I can help," I said.

She looked at me, stunned, and said, "But I have a whole list of arguments ready."

"We can do that, but it's your decision, and you know about selling past the sale," I said.

"Yeah, I know. Once you've made the sale, get out of there; otherwise, you might change the person's mind. Fine, but I'm going to email you my notes anyway," she said, and a big smile came across her face. "I'm pretty excited about this."

"Me, too!" I said. And I was. Not just because I was interested in seeing how The Great Game worked, but because I knew this would help the agency become Rachel's. By implementing a new form of operating, she'd be putting her stamp on the organization and leading us forward her way.

It was 4:45 p.m., and I was just about to pack up and head home. The office was full and busy. The team was working toward an important new business pitch scheduled for next week, and the excitement was palpable. I love those times at an agency when the team is on the hunt for the next great customer.

My phone started to buzz, and I picked it up, seeing it was Matt. "Hey, Matt, what's happening?"

"Not much. You still at the office? It sounds like things are busy there," he said.

"Yep, but I was just about to leave. Trying to get home in time for Danielle's 5:30 soccer game," I said.

"Oh, great. I won't keep you long. I just wanted to see if you had any ideas for me regarding the problems happening at Titan."

"You know, I do. But I'm not yet ready to make a firm suggestion because we're going to try to solve a similar problem at my shop," I said. I filled Matt in on our trip to visit SRC to learn about *The Great Game of Business* and shared our decision earlier that morning to implement The Great Game at our company.

"Huh, that *does* sound interesting. But open-book management? I'm not sure that would work here," he said.

"That appears to be one of the first things people react strongly to. It often stops leaders from trying it, according to Jack Stack. He's SRC's CEO and the one who created The Great Game," I said.

"Well, I'll be interested to hear how it goes. I'm open to just about anything at this point," he said.

"Rachel expects it to take at least three months to implement the program, and even that would be at break-neck speed. But she's amped up to go after it, and we do move fast, so that's the goal. I'll keep you posted as we make progress," I said.

After we hung up, I glanced at the list Rachel had sent me on why we should start The Great Game at our company. The final bullet read: It will allow us to move further toward our Purpose of Inspiring Happiness. That was enough for me.

It was Friday morning, and I was eager to hear how Megan and the team had done with their Values. Exactly as expected, my phone buzzed at 9:00 a.m.

"Hey, Megan!" I said.

"Hey, Will!" she said. "How has your week been?"

"Pretty good, but more importantly, how has *your* week been?"

"SO good! The team just continues to work together, and we're close to being on track with the product launch, which is crazy because I feel like we have barely even started PVTV. But we always remind ourselves of our Purpose and Vision, and several times since last week, we've analyzed our initiatives against the Tenets to make sure we were on the right track. So I guess it's working as it should, but I think even just working together on it and having something that is our *own* has made just as big an impact," she said.

"I love to hear that! I think you are lucky because you have such a stellar team to start with," I said.

"I'm sure that helps, but if you'll remember, we were pretty dysfunctional before we started this process."

"That's true. So, how about those Values?" I asked.

"We went through the process after you left us, doing both the 'modeling' and the 'tough questions' exercises. Those were great ways to dig deep into what Values were most meaningful to us. Honestly, I think I learned a little about myself during that process.

"It wasn't long before we started to see some themes arise, and we were coalescing around three distinct Values. And then the silliest thing happened," she said.

"Oh, what was that?" I asked.

"Well, we eventually wiped the whiteboard clean and wrote the three value statements that we had agreed upon on the board.

And then someone from another team poked his head through the door to ask Q a question. After she answered, he looked up at the board and said, "Are you guys rewriting our Values?"

"I told him that no, we were creating unique Values for our team. And he said, 'Well, you might want to try again, those are just our company Values written a little differently.'"

"No way! So you ended up with the company's Values?" I asked.

"It would appear that way. The guy was right. We compared them to SalesLive's Values, and even though we'd written them differently, they were essentially the same as the company's. We had a big laugh and then agreed that, while it felt like it was a bummer that we did all that work to land in the same place, it was actually better that we were able to use the company's Values."

"I love it, and I can honestly say I've never heard of that happening before," I said. "So how do you feel about your Purpose, Vision, Tenets & Values at this point?"

"I love them. They feel like they're ours authentically. And we came together as a team, just by building them. Does this end our process together?" she asked.

"Yes, I don't think you need me any longer, Megan," I said. "Your task now is to find ways to bring your PVTV to life over time. I'll always be here when you need to bounce an idea around, but you've got the ball now. I'm sure you'll find great ways to use PVTV to motivate your team, and I can't wait to get my team using that new product you're building!"

We talked for a few more minutes and then said our good-byes. I was so happy that PVTV was working to help solve the problems Megan's team was facing. Now I just had to hope that The Great Game of Business was a solution for our team too.

SECTION TWO:
THE GREAT GAME
OF BUSINESS

"Who's ready for the Huddle?" Rachel yelled.

It was Wednesday at 10:00 a.m. For the past six months, our agency had been running The Great Game of Business. The Huddle was always on the same day and time, and it started on time. It was one of our rules.

"As a reminder," Rachel said, "these are the rules: Be on time. Be present. Be curious. And especially on that last one, I want all of you to make sure that what we go over makes sense, and if it doesn't, ask questions! If you aren't sure about something, you can presume other people aren't either."

Rachel was standing at a corner of the office, with our more than 200 employees fanning out among desks and breakout areas. It was the only way we could get everyone together for the Huddle, and it gave the entire thing more of a startup feel.

"Now, who wants to recite our PVTV before we get started?" she asked. We always started our Huddle by going over the rules and our PVTV.

A few dozen hands raised, and Rachel called on a newer employee named Ralph.

"Our Purpose is to Inspire Happiness through positive relationships, impactful work, and doing good. Our Vision is to be the world's best . . . no, hold up . . . to be *sought-after* by the world's best companies for our creative problem-solving. We will do this by . . . attracting and retaining exceptional people, building remarkable products and services, and striving for operational excellence."

He took a deep breath before saying our Values.

"We believe in . . . putting the team first . . . thinking positively, celebrating diversity . . . doing good, and having fun!" He finished, and everyone around him gave him high-fives.

"Ralph, that was wonderful. There was just one tiny mistake. Did anyone catch it?" Rachel said.

Another dozen or so hands went up. Rachel called on someone from our quality assurance team. She pointed out that in the Tenets section, Ralph said "building remarkable products and services." The actual Tenet was "building remarkable products and *experiences.*"

She was right, and Rachel talked for a moment about the importance of words before jumping into the Huddle deck. She also made sure to reinforce the great job Ralph did, recognizing that memorizing the PVTV is hard and publicly reciting it is intimidating.

Since implementing The Great Game, we had worked hard to adjust the Huddle to make it work seamlessly for our organization. While some organizations use a large whiteboard, we decided to create and project a colorful PowerPoint deck for the meeting. The format was flexible and easy to share, so team members could review the information between Huddle sessions if they felt the need.

After going over the rules and our PVTV, we started with a quick review of our monthly Plan of Attack. This part of the Huddle involved setting a monthly goal and measurable action items that we check off throughout the month as we make progress. We found that starting with this step reminded everyone of our most important areas of focus. It helped tremendously with keeping everyone aligned.

Then we moved into a review of the Scorecard, which showed our progress against The Critical Number from an annual perspective and for the current quarter. After that, it was time to cover our Areas of Focus. This section had evolved the most since we started. We were consistently learning from our team members what information was the most critical. Currently, the section consisted of five topics:

Earned Revenue & Project Tracking: A financial review and a deep dive into individual agency projects

Sales & New Business: A look at our sales pipeline and opportunities for team members to help

Team Support: Specific projects or initiatives that need additional assistance

Weekly Game Plan: A review of how we did against last week's game plan, and a look at the game plan for the current week

Announcements: Important company announcements for the week

Sentiment Survey: How our team is feeling about the company and how they're feeling overall in their lives

The Sentiment Survey was a relatively new addition, suggested by a team member a month ago as a way to keep tabs on everyone's mental health.

The Huddle always ran 30 minutes or less (we were careful to respect everyone's time), and it was always full of laughter and cheers. It was easily my favorite time of the week.

"Great job up there," I said to Rachel after everyone dispersed, and she came back to her desk.

"Thanks! It's always easier when we're on target with our goals and likely to give out bonuses," she said.

It had been nine months since we decided to pull the trigger on running The Great Game. Rachel had jumped into it with all the gusto I expected. She and the leadership team spent countless hours learning The Great Game. And as we approached the launch date, they had worked with incredible focus to make The Great Game as useful as possible for our team.

After three months, they were ready to roll it out. There were many prep sessions with team members (we broke them out into groups of 30 or 40 to allow for dialogue), including a deep dive into our financials. At one point, I was sitting in on a prep meeting, and Rachel was going over how an agency model works. As she began talking about the concept of profit, she asked the group, "So who wants to take a stab at what kind of profit margin we shoot for?"

This was the first time many of these team members ever thought about that concept, so I was pretty sure the answers would be entertaining.

Rachel called on a young man who said, "My dad works in the real estate business, and I know the percentage he gets when he sells a house, so I'd guess around three percent."

A woman named Linda chimed in, saying that she was sure it was closer to 60 percent. There were several other guesses, and eventually, Rachel cut them off.

"A solid marketing agency will have between a 15 percent and 20 percent profit margin. Though Linda, maybe we need to move you from creative over to finance so you can help us get that up to 60 percent," she said with a wink.

Listening to that conversation reminded me just how vital this entire process was. Exposing our numbers and trusting our team had become a critical component of our culture, and at this point, I couldn't imagine running any business without it.

But that wasn't always the case. Early on in The Great Game planning, I was one of the people who pushed against open-book management.

"I'm not sure that's the best approach. I know that's what the book says, but exposing all of our numbers to the team?" I said. "I don't think our people are ready for that."

"First of all, we won't be sharing *all* of our numbers, remember. We will show total payroll, but we'll never expose what individuals on the team make. But beyond that, I'd be curious what anyone else thinks," Rachel said, looking at the rest of the leadership team.

Ahmet spoke first. "Well, I'm all for it. As a sales guy, I say anything that will light a fire under the team to see the impact of sales leads is good with me."

"I'm a little worried," said Martha. "What if they share that information outside of the office? We have a big staff. I can't imagine that some of this won't get out."

"What would you be worried could happen if they did share something?" Rachel asked.

"I'll tell you," Steve said. "Our clients might hear that we're struggling and get worried about our stability. I don't need anything making it harder to retain and grow our customers."

"Agreed," chimed in Ahmet. "If we have a big pitch and word gets out that the agency isn't stable, it could hurt our chances at winning the business we need."

Martha shook her head a little and said, "But, Ahmet, you're always coming to me wondering how we can get more of our team members to care about sales. And it's pretty common knowledge that the agency business has ups and downs. We always come out on top in the end, even if it's not always pretty financially at every point in time. Just a few weeks ago, when we were behind on quarterly numbers, you said that if everyone knew the state of our financials, they'd be a lot more likely to get involved."

"Well, that's true," Ahmet admitted.

"And Steve, don't you think if the team knew the profitability of accounts and the impact that makes to our business overall, they'd be more willing to focus on client growth?" Rachel asked.

"I do think that would help. But you can't be saying that word would never leak about our numbers," he said.

Rachel said, "No, of course, I can't. I've wrestled with the possibility as well. Three things helped me get over it. First, we have to trust our team. If we have people we can't trust, they aren't the right people for our company. Second, people could share plenty of things out into the world that could make clients nervous. Remember last week when IT thought they had accidentally wiped all of the media files for Titan?"

"Yeah, that was terrifying. Luckily IT realized the mistake, but people were freaking, including me!" he said.

"Even though nothing bad ended up happening, having that kind of information get out would be far worse than someone sharing that we didn't hit our revenue goal or that our profit dropped to eight percent. My point is, if our team members want to share information that could hurt us, they could do much worse than sharing our financials," Rachel said.

"And what's your third point?" I asked.

"The third is that the pros far outweigh the cons. Martha's right— what we're giving up for a little bit of risk is the opportunity to have a team that gets what we're doing. One that understands how what they do impacts our financials, and one that trusts us more because we're willing to share everything with them.

"And, Will, aren't you always telling us that the most important ingredient in a successful team is trust?" she asked.

"Yeah, good point. Trust is hard to come by and extremely easy to lose, and I admit that sharing our financials would bring an entirely new level of trust into the team," I said.

As we continued to talk about the issue, it became clear that Rachel was right that the pros far outweigh the cons while there were some small risks.

After the discussion, we all agreed to back the move to open-book management fully. We also decided, per Jack's suggestion, to call it open-book *leadership*. An essential aspect of a good team, and especially a good leadership team, is that everyone should speak up and have their points heard, and once a decision is made, everyone agrees and fully backs it.

The last six months of running The Great Game had brought a new kind of energy into the company. The problems Rachel had been experiencing, like people feeling disconnected, in-fighting, and questions about where money was going, had all but disappeared. What was more, employee retention was higher than it had ever been, after it had been dropping to lows we had never experienced.

It was like palpable energy was coursing through the company, and it felt like the old days. The team was coming together in ways I didn't think possible in a larger company.

I shared all of this good news with Charles, who was back from his European cycling trip. He was enthralled with our move to The Great Game.

"So all of your numbers are exposed, other than employee salary?" he asked.

"That's right. We've fully embraced open-book leadership," I said.

"And you have goals set up for the year, broken down by quarter? And everyone is incentivized against those goals, with no personal goals, just team goals?"

"That's right. We're going for a total team environment, so rewarding individuals on their performance even if the company struggles would give team members the wrong goal. Why worry about the team's performance if you can hit your personal goals and get a bonus?" I said.

Charles nodded. "Yes, that's an issue I've seen in my career. Having team members that do a great job in their individual roles but do nothing to help their teammates is a tough dilemma for a team leader."

"Exactly. I want to reorient our company to the big, shared goal and align individual performance with the success of the team," I said.

"I do love that. I always respected the athletes who said they'd trade in all the individual awards to get one more win as a team," he said. "Okay, now tell me a little more about the Huddle."

I explained to him that the Huddle was, for us, really the heartbeat of The Great Game. It was our weekly time to come together, get everyone on the same page, and recharge the team toward the goal. It always provided a jolt of energy into the week.

"I'd love to sit in on one of those at some point. Sounds exciting!" he said. "And what's Jack like?"

"Oh, you'd love him. He's just the kind of leader that you and I respect. No ego; he's all about helping the team succeed. He has a great blend of creating a plan and motivating the team toward it. And he cares about the team members on a personal level. And after meeting him, it made sense that he would create a system like this," I said.

I shared more about how much the culture had changed since we started The Great Game. He commented that it sounded like an incredible way to promote cooperation toward a common goal, giving people more meaning in their jobs.

"Do you think The Game would work at a larger company? I know you were trying to solve problems at your shop because you had grown to over 200 people quickly, but what about much larger businesses?" he asked.

"They have many case studies with large businesses, and I have some firsthand experience with it too. Soon after we implemented the change, I had Matt come to the office to check it out," I said.

"Good old Matt," he said, smiling. "After how you were able to help him with the 5-day turnaround, I'd bet he's up for anything you suggest!"

I laughed. "He said something similar. I had him attend a Huddle, and afterward, we chatted about the process overall. He immediately bought the book and read it in a few days. He embraced the idea right away and hired The Great Game team to help them implement it at Titan. They've been running it for a few months. So far, he says it's been just what he needed."

Charles leaned back in his seat and thought for a moment. "So, how does The Great Game work with PVTV?"

"That's been the most interesting part if you ask me," I said. "At first, we weren't sure if the two were compatible, and if so, how the two approaches could work in concert. We spent a lot of time modeling out ways we could integrate them. Over the last six months, the team has been able to make them work pretty seamlessly together."

"How so? What's an example?" he asked.

"I think of it like this. PVTV is the foundation of our business. It's *why* we do what we do. PVTV helps us remember our aspirations, our high-level plan on how to get there, and the culture we want to have. The Great Game is the playbook for how we'll accomplish those things. It's the day-to-day management system that brings everything together and gives us a real shot at achieving our Vision.

"For example, The Great Game unlocks our ability to Inspire Happiness, which as you know is our company Purpose. We reinforce this idea with our team consistently. How can we Inspire Happiness in ourselves and others if we're not gelling as a team? How can we donate to nonprofits and help them through volunteer time if our business isn't hitting its financial goals? How can we realize our full potential if we're not bringing our team's full power to help address our biggest problems? The Great Game has become the fuel that powers our PVTV," I said.

"I just love that. And it seems obvious! It's almost like PVTV plus The Great Game of Business is the ultimate operating system for a business," he said.

"Exactly. Honestly, I can't even imagine running PVTV without The Great Game. It's almost like they were meant to work together."

Standing outside the SalesLive office, I went over my game plan.

1. **Step one:** Walk right up to Rosey and tell her that William is here to see Megan.
2. **Step two:** Thank her politely.
3. **Step three:** Make hilarious robot-based jokes.
4. **Step four:** Walk away before she can respond.

When Megan and I set up the meeting, I asked her if Rosey was back in business.

She reminded me that Rosey wasn't her real name (and I reminded her that she'll always be Rosey to me) and that, yes, she was working the front desk once more. I was ready to work my plan.

Taking a deep breath and summoning some courage, I walked through the doors and entered the lobby. I spotted Rosey in her usual place, with her fake notepad in front of her.

I marched right up to her and said, "Hi, I'm Will and . . . I mean, I'm *William*, and I have a 9:00 a.m. appointment with Megan."

She looked down, pretending to check her notepad, and said, "Yes, thank you. I see your appointment here. I will let her know. You can take a seat over on one of those couches."

"Thank you very much," I said. The time had come for some jokes.

"What do you call a pirate robot?"

She looked up at me, eyes blinking.

"'*Arrrrr*2-D2'! Get it? What does R2-D2 use to open PDF files?"

More blinking eyes.

"'AdobeWan Kenobi'! Okay, why did the robot marry his fiancée? He couldn't resistor!"

Still nothing. Last chance.

"Okay, why is a robot mechanic never lonely?" I waited for a beat, then said, "Because he's always making new friends."

I then turned and walked over to the couch and sat down. I looked over at Rosey. Honestly, I was a bit deflated that she hadn't reacted. Danielle had said my robot jokes were hilarious. Rosey was still looking in the same direction, eyes blinking.

Suddenly I heard a loud, "Ha!" I looked over at Rosey and saw her mouth open and another "Ha!" come out.

Then she started laughing. Her head tilted back and her mouth opened wide and a cascading "Ha-ha-ha!" came out of her soundbox.

Just then, Megan came around the corner and made her way over to me, looking at Rosey with a confused look on her face. "What is wrong with her? Maybe she needs to go back to the shop."

I shrugged and said, "Who knows, but I think I like this new and improved Rosey."

As we exited the lobby and made our way into the main area, we could still hear Rosey laughing in the background. Mission accomplished.

Megan led us toward a meeting area she'd set up. I sat down on a small sofa, and she pulled a few whiteboards near us.

"Just creating some cover for our chat," she said as she maneuvered the whiteboards to form a little barrier.

"So, how have you been?" I asked.

"I was trying to think, how long has it been since we talked?" she asked.

"Maybe three months?"

"That sounds right," she said. "Wow. So much has happened since then. As you know, we had a killer product launch!"

"Yes, I heard SEAL Team X was a huge success," I said, joking about the pet name we had given her team.

"We did pretty well," she said, laughing. "I had forgotten about that name. Our product launch ended up being the most successful in company history. In fact, after how well that rollout went, Shera decided to promote our team to lead Product Development!"

"Woah! That's amazing! I did hear that, and what's more, I heard you're leading the team!" I exclaimed. Shera had reached out to me when she was considering this move, asking for my opinion of Megan, given the time we had spent together. I told her if she didn't promote her into that spot, I would steal her away for my team.

"I sure am! And now I have almost 75 employees that report to me. I still can't quite believe it," she said.

"I'm curious. Did you create a new PVTV for the team?"

She explained that her leadership team, which she kept intact, spent time discussing whether the PVTV from their previous team would work. As it turned out, what they created for SEAL Team X worked perfectly for the Product Team overall.

It was refreshing to be able to keep the original PVTV that we all feel so connected to," she said.

She walked up to the whiteboard and wrote:

SalesLive Purpose

To eliminate the tension between salespeople and their prospects

Product Team Purpose

To strengthen the relationship between salespeople and their clients

SalesLive Vision

To be the ultimate tool for our customers to achieve their sales goals

Product Team Vision

To be the most indispensable tool in the salesperson's toolbox

SalesLive Tenets

We will do this by putting the customer first, believing in each other, and focusing on profitable growth

Product Team Tenets

We will do this by maximizing our strengths as a team, always keeping the salesperson in mind, and focusing on quality over quantity

SalesLive Values

We believe in being all for one and one for all, gaining advantage, and always being two steps ahead

Product Team Values

We believe in being all for one and one for all, gaining advantage, and always being two steps ahead

"All of that sounds wonderful," I said.

"It was . . . well, it is . . . but, well, something's just not right," she said. "I can't quite put my finger on it, but things feel like they're starting to fall apart."

Her body language changed immediately. The peppy, positive energy she showed up until that point was gone.

Continuing, she said, "At the beginning, everyone seemed pumped about the new team structure and our PVTV. But lately, I've heard rumors that some people are upset about their place in the team, and others feel like they aren't doing anything meaningful to help the team overall. There seems to be a mood of disconnectedness. That's the best way I think I can describe it."

I thought for a moment and then said, "Tell me how you bring your Purpose, Vision, Tenets & Values to life. Maybe that's a place we can look for answers."

"Sure. First off, we start every meeting by reciting our PVTV. Per your suggestion, my leadership team and I have memorized it word for word," she said.

"How long did that take, by the way?" I asked.

Laughing, she said, "Well, it was easy for some of the team members, but a few were pretty grumpy about it. A couple of them wrote it on a Post-it and put it on their mirror at home, so every morning when they were getting ready, they could read it. Many of us would recite it while driving into the office. I still do that often, afraid that I'll forget a word one day in front of the team!"

"I love those examples," I said. "My team even went so far as to create a physical device that helped them remember our Values. For 'Team First,' the team points their index finger up. And for 'Think Positively,' they point to their head. These tricks helped them remember the Values, and now we all have a laugh when someone does them."

"Ha! That's fun," she said. "I'll give you a few examples of how we implement each of the components of PVTV. For our Purpose, we always make sure to come back to it when we have a big decision to make. I'll often challenge our team on an idea to ask them if it will strengthen the relationship between our salespeople and their clients. It's a great device to create clarity around big decisions.

"We use our Vision as our guide on a daily, weekly, and monthly basis. Our goal as a team is to be the most indispensable tool in the salesperson's toolbox. I ask at each of our weekly leadership team meetings if we're making progress toward that goal. And we've started to find ways to measure our Vision, which I think is important. If we don't do that, I don't think we'll know if we're making progress. Actually, the one thing I think is missing from PVTV is a way to measure how well we're doing with it and because of it. That might be something to think about," she said.

I nodded in agreement. "It's funny you say that. Back when we first started working together, I struggled with how to measure PVTV too. Quite frankly, when I started thinking about it, I was a bit shocked that I had never really considered that piece. We started running *The Great Game of Business*, and now we measure every aspect of our PVTV!"

"Oh, wow. I'd love to hear more about that. I read the book when you gave it to me, and I'm pretty interested in The Great Game overall," she said.

It occurred to me that maybe Megan could rectify her problems by implementing The Great Game along with their PVTV. It had worked for my agency and Titan, but as a company overall. I wondered if it would work for a team to implement the combination.

"Shall I continue with the examples?" Megan asked.

"Oh, yes, sorry. I was just thinking about something that might be interesting to consider. Please continue. How do you use your Tenets?" I asked.

"Okay, and when we're done talking about Tenets, let's circle back to The Great Game. As you taught us, the Tenets are the things we need to do to achieve our Vision. So, in a sense, they're the actual playbook on what we should be focusing on. That's why we decided to structure our weekly all-team meeting around our Tenets. The first section of the meeting is our first Tenet, 'Maximizing our strengths as a team.' We talk about how the team is doing, if people are working on products that align with their skills, and whether or not the team is optimized. Then we move into our second Tenet, 'Always keep the salesperson in mind.' This point is where we discuss customer feedback, look at user trends, and discuss what needs we're seeing that our products could fulfill with our customers. And the final section of our weekly meeting is based on our third Tenet, 'Focus on quality over quantity.' During this part of the meeting, we talk about how we can focus more and slow down. We question unrealistic deadlines and debate the merits of additional functionality in our products.

"Running our meetings against our Tenets has kept us focused as a team and ensures that we keep our overall Vision in mind as we go through the week," she said.

"I assume there are also times when you can use your Tenets to help guide the team toward a decision," I said.

"Absolutely. It's gotten to the point where most people will point out how an idea they're advocating for aligns with one of our Tenets. The ideas that win usually make sense across all three."

There was a knock on the door, and Q poked her head in.

"Oh, hi Will! Sorry to interrupt you guys. Megan, I have a quick question for you," she said.

Megan said, "No problem. Why don't you come on in for a minute? I have something I'd like to ask you as well."

Q came in and asked Megan her question. Megan considered the question for a moment and then asked Q what she thought was the right path to take. When Q told her, Megan agreed.

"Now, I'd like you to help me with something," Megan said. "I'm walking Will through how we bring our PVTV to life. I was just about to talk about our Values when you stopped by. Would you share with him the idea you came up with for our monthly meetings?"

"You bet!" Q said and turned to me. "We were trying to figure out how to bring our Values to life, and the idea struck me that rather than having the leadership team recognize team members for exhibiting our Values, it would make more sense to have their peers recognize them. We went through several concepts and ultimately ended up with our Monthly Heroes. We conducted a vote to have everyone on the team nominate someone for each of our three Values. They needed to describe how they thought each person embodied the Value.

"At each monthly all-hands team meeting, we announce the three winners. They are our Monthly Heroes. Then, at the next monthly meeting, that Hero gets to nominate someone else for that Value. It's great fun, and it allows us to remember and remind each other of our Values," she said.

"I love that! Peer recognition is important and so powerful," I said.

"Plus," Megan added, "the giver and the receiver end up feeling great, which is a bonus."

We both thanked Q for sharing, and she left to get back to work.

"I just wanted to point something out about your interaction with Q when she asked you for advice," I said. "I noticed that you didn't answer the question for her but rather asked her what she thought was the right answer."

Megan nodded. "That's actually something that I learned from Shera. I kept finding myself solving my team's problems, and I was overwhelmed with their constant need for my help. Then I had a meeting with Shera about something different, and as she redirected the question back to me to answer, I realized that she had always done that. Because I knew she would do that, I spent time thinking about what the best answer might be before asking for her help. Once I started trying that with my team, everything changed. Now, it's rare that I have to give them an answer at all."

"It's such a smart leadership tactic," I said. "And hopefully, that same tactic can be embraced by your leadership team members when they interact with their team members."

"Oh, that's a great idea. I can't believe I never thought of sharing that," she said as she made a note in her notebook.

"Okay, so based on how we bring our PVTV to life, do you have any insight into why we might be struggling right now?" she asked.

"Well, first off, you're doing a great job bringing your PVTV to life. I'm impressed that you could find so many ways to involve each element in the team's day-to-day workflow. So, I don't think your struggles have to do with that," I said.

I explained that many of her team's problems were similar to those that my agency and Titan had faced earlier in the year.

"Both of our companies were struggling with a lack of motivation, a sense of disconnectedness, and an overall lack of people feeling that they weren't part of a team, that they were a cog in a machine," I said.

"And how are things now?" she asked.

"Things have never been better! Morale is up, and productivity is off the charts. Employee retention has never been higher. Basically, we're running better than I ever thought possible!" I said.

"So, what changed?" Megan asked.

"I learned that PVTV is a terrific way to create a foundational level of focus, but on its own, it can't bring a team together in a meaningful, measurable way. It doesn't create an operating model for success. When I put PVTV together with *The Great Game of Business*, I saw the team's real potential," I said.

"Wow, that's a powerful statement," she said.

"I know. Honestly, I can't see running a business ever again without this new model. I'm thinking of it as the ultimate operating system for a business," I said.

"Do you think it could work for my team?" she asked.

"Well, the problems you are experiencing definitely are ones that we were able to correct with this new model. But it's only ever been done at a company level. I'd have to think about how it could work for a team within a company," I said, scratching my chin.

"If you'd be willing to try, I'd be willing to be the guinea pig!" she said.

I thought about that for a moment. If PVTV plus *The Great Game of Business* could work for a team, it would be magical. We'd have to tweak certain things to make it less company-focused and more team-focused, but I didn't see why that would be too hard to work through. Plus, I could use Rachel to help. She'd essentially become the world's foremost expert on the approach.

"Okay, you know what? Let's do it! I think there's potential for this to work for teams as well as businesses, and I can't think of a better team to try it with than SEAL Team X," I said.

Megan and I spent the rest of our time together talking about what the process might be. I gathered notes so I could speak with Rachel. I said I'd share the plan with her once Rachel and I had worked it out. Megan agreed to have her leadership team read *The Great Game of Business*. With our to-do lists in place, we set a date for two weeks out for our first meeting.

I said I'd show myself out. As I made my way through the lobby, I was deep in thought about this new challenge. I almost bumped into Rosey.

"Oh, sorry about that. I didn't see you there," I said to her.

She looked up at me, blinked a few times, and said, "Hello, William." A big grin showed on her face.

It had been a good day.

"Another challenge, huh?" Rachel smiled. "I think you're kind of addicted to these turnarounds."

I laughed. "Rach, you aren't wrong. Do you think it would work?"

"Well, of course, I do! I mean, figuring out how to make it work for a team instead of a company will be interesting, but it's certainly doable," she said. "The power of your PVTV methodology working in partnership with Jack's Great Game system has done wonders for our agency. They complement each other so well. I don't see why we can't make it work for a team."

"We?" I asked.

"Uh, there's no chance I'm going to miss out on participating! I want to see how this works. Plus, I'm pretty sure no one on the planet knows more about how to put PVTV together with The Great Game better than I do."

She was right about that. I knew she'd be tremendously helpful, but I was worried about putting more on her plate. She's entirely dedicated to her work. Most of my worries for her are that she's overworking and putting too much pressure on herself. Adding more to her already heavy workload wasn't at the top of my list.

"No doubt I could use your help, but let's be careful about how much of your time we use for this. I'm sure we'll find some opportunities for you to be part of the meetings, and for sure, you can help me create the game plan," I said.

She agreed, and we began talking about how to break down The Great Game in a way that would allow us to streamline Megan's implementation of it. After about twenty minutes of discussing and referencing both *The Great Game of Business* and *Get in the Game* books, Rachel walked to the whiteboard and wrote:

Meeting 1: Introducing The Great Game	**ALWAYS**
Meeting 2: Budget and The Critical Number	**CONNECT**
Meeting 3: The Huddle and Scoreboard	**TO PVTV**
Meeting 4: MiniGames and Early Wins	
Meeting 5: Involving the Team	

"So here's what we have. You start with explaining The Great Game to the leadership team. After that meeting, you walk through creating The Critical Number. A lot of work has to be done in this step because the team might not have a complete budget," she said.

"That's so right. In fact, Megan told me that they don't even have a budget," I said.

"Really?" Rachel asked.

"Yeah, that was my first reaction, too. But think about it, does our Creative Team have its own budget?"

She shook her head. "No, I guess not. How interesting. So, how do they run The Great Game without a financial budget?"

"I've thought about that a lot since meeting with Megan. Some teams would have a budget, in which case they'd work through that process of The Great Game. But many will not. They'll need to focus instead on the most important metrics for their team, whatever they are. I see it as creating a non-financial budget, more metrics-driven, that leads up to The Great Game. It will be fun to experiment to put that together with her," I said.

"Makes sense. That's a meeting I'd like to join. Once those metrics are set, Megan will want to walk the team through the Huddle and create a Scoreboard. As soon as that is locked down, it's important to work with them on MiniGames and ways to find easy, early wins to build momentum and show people how The Great Game works. Actually, that's another meeting I'd like to attend if that's all right," she said.

"Of course. And then we'll end the process with a big kickoff with the entire team. To me, the most important aspect of all of this is what you wrote here," I said, tapping my marker on the words ALWAYS CONNECT TO PVTV. "We have to make sure that we're building on the foundation of PVTV that they already have in place. How does The Great Game reinforce their team's Purpose? In what ways do their Vision and Tenets overlap with their Game? How should the Values dictate behavior while they play the Game?

"And," I added, "are there any conflicting elements of each? At the end of this process, it needs to be obvious how The Great Game and PVTV work seamlessly together and how they're integral to the success of each."

We spent a little more time working on the schedule, once again creating a weekly cadence of meetings. I was sure that Megan's team could move fast, given how quickly they moved through PVTV, but we could always adjust during the process if need be.

INTRODUCING THE GREAT GAME

The team—Q, Sasha, Hala, Ashley, Dustin, and Megan—was assembled in the conference room. It had been two weeks since Megan and I had come up with this plan, and I noticed each of her team members had the book, *The Great Game of Business*, in front of them. Many with dog-eared pages and highlighted passages.

After we caught up for a few minutes, I jumped in.

"Okay, let's get started. I see that you all read the book on The Great Game. Tell me what you thought."

Dustin said, "I really liked the story. What Jack and his team did to turn SRC around was so inspiring."

"I agree! What a phenomenal story," added Ashley.

Sasha said, "For sure, the story was great. But, if we're planning on using this model for our team, I'm not sure I get it."

"How do you mean?" I asked.

"Well, we don't have access to the financials the way this model seems to require. I don't see how it would work without that," he said.

"Also, we're a software company, not a manufacturing company," added Hala. "I had a hard time relating to much of the workflow the book lays out."

"Plus, we're a team, not an entire company. This model seems to be for a company to use," said Q.

I smiled. These were all aspects of The Great Game that I assumed they would have a difficult time wrapping their heads around.

"All good points," I said. "Let's start with the easy one. Yes, you're a software company, and that's very different from SRC. However, my agency, which is a services company, runs The Game quite effectively. So I have no doubt I can show you how to adapt it to work for your team.

"In terms of the financials, this was something that I realized pretty quickly as well. We will be adapting the Game a little in order to make sure it can work without the financial rigor typically required. I have some thoughts, but we'll get into that as we move through the process," I said.

"And what about the fact that we're a team and not a company?" asked Q.

"Aha. That," I said, "is going to be our focus. How do we make The Great Game work for a team at a company that doesn't yet run The Great Game? That's our challenge, and I'm excited to tackle it with you all."

"How does this work with our PVTV?" asked Hala.

"Glad you asked. Both my agency and Titan have figured out ways to bring these two business philosophies together to magnify the power of each. At the end of our work together, the goal is for your team to be running PVTV and *The Great Game of Business* together to unlock your team's full potential. And if any team can do it, I know this team can."

I walked up the whiteboard and drew the diagram from the book:

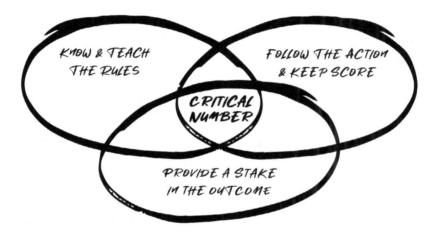

"Today, we're going to talk about The Great Game overall, focusing on these three core concepts: Know & Teach the Rules, Follow the Action & Keep Score, and Provide a Stake in the Outcome. The important thing is to remember why The Great Game is central to a company or team's success. You've all read the book. What do you think the power of The Great Game is?"

Megan said, "I think it's the ability to bring people together to really feel like a team. It seems like running The Game can make the team more aligned and more trusting."

"I agree. I'd add that it also gives you a way to measure progress and work toward a common goal together," said Ashley.

"Yeah, it reminds everybody what we're supposed to be working on day to day and how that ladders up," said Dustin.

"Exactly! You guys get it," I said. "I've never seen anything in business bring a group of people closer together than The Great Game. What drew me to it initially was that it creates a comradery that you don't usually see in business. Typically you only see it in sports.

"The first thing we'll need to do is make sure we understand The Great Game and that we are always educating the broader team about it. We'll suggest that everyone read the book, but not everyone will. Those who do will have similar questions to what you shared with me earlier. Continuous education of the Game is going to be a priority. When we roll it out, we'll have a big meeting with everyone to explain how it works. While you might think it makes perfect sense, you have to remember that you will have been working on it for weeks, whereas they're just learning about it," I said.

I explained that *The Great Game of Business* book would expose everything the team is doing, why they're doing it, and focus everyone on the same goals. All of that ultimately rolls up to The Critical Number.

"What's The Critical Number?" asked Q.

"The Critical Number is the ultimate way your team will define success. It is a metric that, if you achieve it, everything else takes care of itself. The Critical Number is essentially the focus of The Game," I said.

I asked her to hand me her book, and I thumbed through it for a second until I found the page I was looking for.

"Here it is. The book describes The Critical Number as 'an operational or financial number that represents a weakness or vulnerability that if not addressed and corrected will negatively impact the overall performance and long-term security of the business.' You want to make sure that The Critical Number is something everyone thinks they can affect."

"How will we come up with The Critical Number?" Dustin asked.

"We're going to work on that in our next meeting together," I said. "Part of it will be working with the entire team to come up with The Critical Number. Our goal is to get people thinking like owners, and as such, we must treat them like owners and ask for their input."

"I don't know how we'll make them feel like owners. We won't be able to give them equity in the company the way Jack did with SRC," Ashley said.

"That's true," I said. "However, it's not required that people have equity in order to feel invested in the place they work. I've seen plenty of companies where people have stock in their company yet still don't act like owners. And I'd argue that each of you on this leadership team feels a strong connection to the company at this point. Am I wrong?"

Everyone nodded their heads, and Megan said, "I certainly do, and I think it's because we've worked so closely together on the

PVTV for our team. So you think the combination of PVTV and The Great Game will help the rest of our team feel like we do?"

"I definitely do. I've seen it work at my company. We don't have an equity program, mostly because we do not have plans to sell the company, but through The Great Game specifically, we now can share in the success of the company with everyone on the team," I said.

"The next aspect of The Great Game, after we've learned the rules, is to Follow the Action and Keep Score. Every week you will run what we call the Huddle, which is when everyone comes together to review progress against The Critical Number. Is there a place in the office where we can set up our Huddle area? We'd need a wall big enough to put the Scoreboard and enough room for your entire team to gather around for the weekly Huddle," I said.

"We have a spot," said Megan.

"Great! Let's meet there for our next meeting. The idea is to have an area where people can see the current 'Score.' Typically, this is done with a large scoreboard that shows progress. This display is also where we'll highlight any MiniGames you might be running. You all read about MiniGames, correct?" I asked.

Hala said, "Yes, they seemed like the most fun part of The Game!"

"They definitely can be," I said. "Okay, so we've talked about the education portion of The Game. Let's talk about Providing a Stake in the Outcome. As you read the book, how did SRC provide a stake in the Outcome for its employees?"

"Employees were given a percentage of the profit, essentially," Megan said.

"That's right. Did any of you have ideas of how your team might be given a stake in the Outcome?" I asked.

"Does it have to be monetary?" Sasha asked.

"I think it does," I said. "MiniGame rewards can be all sorts of things, like pizza parties, new office equipment, or gift cards. But the reward at the end of the Game does need to be financial, in my opinion."

"We don't run our P&L, so we can't tie the reward to profit exactly," said Megan. "But I could talk to Shera about a bonus pool that, if the success of the team were enough, she'd probably agree to."

"That would be great, and I'm sure if the team performs as well as we hope they will, that would be a no-brainer for Shera," I said.

We talked for a bit longer about setting up the bonus plan, but we would need to know how the Game would run before we could do too much planning on that.

I walked back up to the whiteboard and said, "Okay, so now that we understand the high-level elements of the Game, let me show you the process we will go through from this point:

Meeting 1: Introducing The Great Game	**ALWAYS CONNECT TO PVTV**
Meeting 2: The Critical Number	
Meeting 3: The Huddle and Scoreboard	
Meeting 4: MiniGames and Quick Wins	
Meeting 5: The First Huddle	

"Okay, our first meeting is done. At the next meeting, we will work on determining The Critical Number. The meeting after that, we will spend time on the elements of the weekly Huddle. That will include developing the Scoreboard. In our fourth meeting, we will work on some initial ideas for MiniGames and look at some quick wins to build momentum for the team. And the final meeting will be when we roll everything out to the team. Any questions?"

Sasha asked, "I see that you wrote 'always connect to PVTV' on the right. What do you mean by that?"

"I want to make sure that throughout this process, we are keeping our PVTV in mind. Remember, our goal is to create a new operating system for your team, built on two components: PVTV and *The Great Game of Business*. Each of them must complement each other and work in concert to build the strength and success of your team. While we'll be focusing mostly on the Game in these meetings, we should always make sure we are infusing it with your already developed PVTV," I said.

I shared a few more thoughts about the upcoming meetings and told them Rachel would join for most of them. I positioned her as an expert in all of this work. The team seemed excited, even if a little overwhelmed. I could hardly blame them. This information was a lot to throw at them all at once, but I had a feeling they would take to it quickly.

The fact that they had already embraced (and were living) their PVTV made me hopeful that this would work. The nine months or so since they had rolled out their PVTV was likely just enough time to make sure they had it fully entrenched into their team. I doubt implementing *The Great Game of Business* could be done much sooner after a team's PVTV creation.

THE CRITICAL NUMBER

"So this is SalesLive," Rachel said as we exited the Lyft.

"I forgot that you've never been here," I said. "I think they moved into this office a year or two ago. It's massive, right?"

"Sure is. I like these funky old converted warehouses. Maybe we should think about that when our lease is up in a few years," she said.

We made our way through the entryway and found ourselves in a short line waiting to check in.

"I'm pretty excited to be on one of your adventures," she said. I looked at her, and she had a smirk on her face. Seeing my look of doubt, she quickly added, "No, really! Thanks for having me along to help."

"Well, really! At this point, you're the expert, so I wouldn't dream of doing it without you," I said.

It was our turn to check in with Rosey. My favorite robot looked up from her clipboard and said, "William, how have you been?"

"Great to see you!" I said. "I'm glad you remembered me. I was worried your skills were getting a little . . . *rusty.*"

She looked up at me and blinked several times, and a big smile came across her face. She reached out her fist, and I bumped it. No explosions.

Rachel said, "Hi, my name is—" but before she could finish,

Rosey pointed to the couch and said, "Please sit over there. Megan will be out shortly."

We walked over and sat down, and Rachel said, "Did I do something wrong? She was so friendly with you."

"Don't worry. It's not you," I said. "Rosey takes time to warm up to people. Trust me."

A few minutes later, Megan came into the lobby. We exchanged greetings, and Rachel asked her if it was always this busy at their office.

"Oh, no, it's usually quite quiet in terms of visitors. Today's different because we are giving a bunch of thought leadership talks to our top clients. Actually, Will, how long will we be meeting today? I'm supposed to be speaking to them at 11:00 a.m."

"We'll be done well before that. We're just setting the stage today. Most of the hard work on The Critical Number will come throughout the week between you and your team," I said.

She led us past the conference room we usually used for our meetings to a corner of the large, open space. She had walled off the area with giant whiteboards and set up plenty of seating.

"This is where we decided it would be best for our team to have our Great Game meetings," Rachel said. "We quartered it off for some privacy, and we should be able to keep it as ours for the foreseeable future."

"It's perfect," I said. "And I love that it's public enough to the rest of the company. I expect they'll get curious about what kind of schemes you and the team are cooking up over here."

Megan's team was seated at a table near the whiteboard wall. They looked ready to go.

After I introduced Rachel to the gang, I kicked things off.

"Today, we're going to focus on The Critical Number. Before we get started, can someone tell me the three core areas of The Great Game of Business that we went over in our last meeting?"

Hala said, "I think I can. The first component is education. We need to make sure everyone knows the rules and the core metrics. I believe the second part was following the action and keeping score through things like the Huddle and MiniGames. And the third . . ."

She hesitated, not able to remember point three. Sasha jumped in, "The third was providing a stake in the outcome, so people have something to work for, and we're all rewarded for hitting the team's goals."

"Great! And nice teamwork. You can think of those three concepts as thinking like an owner, acting like an owner, and feeling like an owner," I said.

"So today, we'll talk about The Critical Number. Our next meeting will focus on the Huddle and Scoreboard. After that, we'll knock out the concept of MiniGames and how to get Quick Wins. And then all we have to do is roll it out to the team in our final meeting. Sounds easy, right?" I said, obviously joking with the last bit.

"Sure, just completely change everything we're doing," Megan said, laughing. "We got this."

"I know you do. Okay, Rachel, do you want to kick us off?" I asked.

"You bet. Thanks, Will. And before I start, I want to encourage you. We've gone through this exercise of implementing The Great Game alongside PVTV. If we can do it, I have no doubt this team can do it too."

She walked up to the whiteboard and wrote:

THE CRITICAL NUMBER

STEP 1: Annual Success Metrics

STEP 2: Supporting, Trackable Data

STEP 3: Major Weaknesses

STEP 4: Critical Number (Financial, Marketplace, Operational, People)

(REMEMBER YOUR PVTV)

She said, "It's important to point out that today we're going to go over the process, but you'll do the real work after this meeting. It is critical—pun intended—that you bring everyone on your team into the process.

"You'll start by making sure you have a firm grasp on your annual success metrics. For a business, that will likely be some combination of top-line revenue and annual profit. For a team like yours, it may be different. If your team has Profit & Loss accountability, then this will be pretty straightforward. But I understand your team does not have a P&L, correct?" Rachel asked.

"Not yet," Megan said.

"Okay, no worries. So you'll want to spend time, if you haven't already, figuring out what your big goal is for the year. Maybe it's launching a certain product or hitting a goal number of customers using your suite of products. This metric will inform how you set up the Game, and everything will flow from what you decide, so take your time with it. Make sense?"

Everyone nodded, so she continued.

"Once you know what your annual success metric is, you'll work to create a list of supporting, trackable data that you can apply to it. These points will operate similarly to the way your Tenets work with your Vision. Break down everything you can track that will make an impact on the big goal."

"Can you give us an example?" asked Q.

"Absolutely. Let's assume your goal at the end of this year is to hit 1,000 customers using your product," she said.

"More like 10,000," Dustin said.

"Okay, even better. So your goal is to get to 10,000 customers. Throw out some things you'd need to measure to help you get to that goal."

The team started lobbing data points at Rachel: customer

satisfaction scores, customer churn, product defects, and marketing acquisition.

After they started to lose steam, Rachel said, "Great, so in just a few minutes, you listed off almost 20 things you could measure. That's the idea.

"The third part of the process is to start thinking about the current weaknesses of the team that will hurt your chances of hitting the goal. There's a good chance you will find those within the list we just went over. For instance, someone mentioned customer churn. How do you define that here?"

Ashley said, "Customer churn is the frequency at which customers stop being customers. If we have 100 customers and six leave over the course of a month, then our churn rate is six percent."

"Great, so that's a terrific number to measure because it directly impacts the goal of hitting 10,000 customers. Now, as you think about weaknesses, you might realize that, right now, your churn rate is too high. If so, that would be something you'd put on the list. Everyone with me?" she asked.

Everyone nodded.

"By this point, the last step should be pretty easy. You'll identify the one thing this year that you need to focus on improving beyond anything else. Something that everyone can affect, and something that will help you achieve the big goal if you focus everyone's attention on it."

I spoke up, "Keep in mind that a good Critical Number will make your team stronger by eliminating weakness and supporting the annual goal. And it's a bonus when The Critical Number also educates your team members about the business. For instance, my guess is not many people on your team know the importance of customer churn. They might not even know the term. The more they're learning about how the team and business work, the better."

"Great point, Will. And while you decide what your Critical Number should be, I bought a printout of some questions you can use as a guide," Rachel said.

She passed around a one-page document.

CRITICAL NUMBER WORKSHEET

1. *Is The Critical Number feasible?*

   a. *Does the team have (or can they get) the resources, skills, time, and support needed to achieve The Critical Number?*

2. *Is The Critical Number impactful?*

   a. *Goal impact: Will The Critical Number keep people focused on achieving the annual goal?*

   b. *Strategic impact: Will The Critical Number make the team stronger and healthier by eliminating weaknesses and growing strategically?*

   c. *Educational impact: Will The Critical Number help educate people about the different aspects of the team and business and teach people exactly what it takes to succeed?*

3. *Is The Critical Number timely?*

    a. *Does The Critical Number represent something that needs to be done now, or do other things need to be done first?*

    b. *Does it need to be done before things worsen or the window closes?*

"I see this talks about timeliness," Q said.

"That's right," I said. "You'll likely have a different Critical Number each year, depending on what is most important to address within the business."

"I suggest you go through all of this as a leadership team first and then walk the rest of the team through it. Let people poke holes and make suggestions to any aspect of it," Rachel said.

They had a few more questions after that, but by and large, they seemed to grasp the concept.

Megan walked us out, and as Rachel and I waited for the Lyft to arrive, I said, "Great job in there. Between your explanation and the fact that they read the book, *The Great Game of Business*, I think they pretty well understand what to do."

"Yes, I'm sure reading the book helped, and while I appreciate the recognition of my incredible teaching abilities—"

"Did I say 'incredible'?" I joked.

"You implied it," she laughed. "Seriously, though, I think the reason they're so into the process and picking it up so quickly is because they went through the PVTV process already. They're acting like a focused, well-aligned, trusting team already. I can't think of a better primer to get ready for The Great Game than to develop and bring to life your PVTV."

THE HUDDLE AND SCOREBOARD

"Okay, so how did last week's Critical Number exercise go?" Rachel asked after everyone had greeted each other.

We were once again seated in the team's area by the whiteboard wall.

Megan spoke first, "We started just as you suggested, focusing on the annual success metrics. While we don't control our P&L, we still could identify many metrics that defined our success. Those are listed there."

She pointed toward a section of the whiteboard with a list of metrics expected from a product team. It included customer satisfaction results, deadline achievement, and quality of delivery.

"Then we broke into teams and worked on creating trackable supporting data for each of those metrics. I would say each success metric has around four data points that we can use to track our progress," Megan said.

"That was a great exercise," Q said. "It was the first time that I had even thought about measuring some of the things we do. It sounds silly to say that, but it made me question why we do certain things."

"We had the same thing happen," Rachel said. "There were things that we were doing at the agency that Will had put in place when he founded the organization. They made sense at that time but had since lost their usefulness for our business."

"I would say the hardest bit for this team was figuring out our major weaknesses," Megan said. "We all work so hard to make this the best team it can be. We own our strengths and our weaknesses but connecting the weaknesses to people made for some awkward conversations. I was proud of how willing everyone was to have the conversation."

Sasha said, "I got a little defensive at the start, and I appreciate you guys sticking with me. Being over Delivery is a tough role because the success of my team relies on everyone else doing their job."

"Did Delivery make its way onto the weaknesses list?" I asked.

"Yep. It was a contender for our Critical Number, actually. We've missed multiple deadlines over the last three months, so I knew it was an issue," he said.

"Ultimately, though," Megan said, "We decided that, while improving Delivery was something we needed to focus on, it wasn't the most critical aspect this year. After we went through all of the options, it was pretty unanimous what the right Critical Number was for us."

She stood up and wrote on the whiteboard:

CRITICAL NUMBER: Customer Retention

"At the end of the day, every weakness we listed pointed toward one glaring problem. We are bleeding out customers. We define customer retention as the percentage of customers that re-sign with us after their annual agreement finishes. Our company was usually around 85 percent in past years, which is very high for our industry. But over the last year, that number has dropped to 75 percent," Megan said.

"What are the main reasons you think the drop happened?" Rachel asked.

"Oh, we don't have to guess," said Q. "Every customer fills out a satisfaction survey when they re-sign or drop off. We reviewed the collected feedback and realized it was an almost identical match to the weaknesses we had listed!"

"What do you think?" Megan asked Rachel.

"I think it's perfect! And the goal is to focus on that number for the next 12 months. Hopefully, you'll make great progress and be able to shift your focus to another Critical Number next year," Rachel said.

"How did it go when you met with the team to walk them through all of this?" I asked.

"It was interesting," Ashley said. "I think they were kind of overwhelmed. We hit them with a lot of information all at once."

"But at the end of it, everyone seemed totally into the idea that our Critical Number would be to improve our customer retention. We even did a little Q&A and asked people to suggest how they could affect the number," Dustin added.

Megan's team gave examples of how their team members answered the question. By and large, everyone could easily point to how they could directly impact The Critical Number.

"That's absolutely terrific, you guys," Rachel said. She stood up and wrote on the whiteboard:

Meeting 1: Introducing The Great Game

Meeting 2: The Critical Number

Meeting 3: The Huddle and Scoreboard

Meeting 4: MiniGames and Quick Wins

Meeting 5: The First Huddle

ALWAYS

CONNECT

TO PVTV

"Before we move on, let's go back to your PVTV and make sure that The Critical Number aligns well with it. Would someone please write your PVTV on the board?"

Hala said, "I'd like to give it a go."

She stood up and wrote:

Product Team Purpose

To strengthen the relationship between salespeople and their clients

Product Team Vision

To be the most indispensable tool in the salesperson's toolbox

Product Team Tenets

We will do this by maximizing our strengths as a team, always keeping the salesperson in mind, and focusing on quality over quantity

Product Team Values

We believe in being all for one and one for all, gaining advantage, and always being two steps ahead

Everyone clapped, and Hala gave a mock curtsy.

"Great job," Rachel said, chuckling. "Okay, who wants to tell me how your Critical Number helps you achieve your Purpose?"

"Clearly, a great indicator of whether we're accomplishing our Purpose to strengthen the relationship that our customer has with their clients is if they value us enough to continue working with us. So I think customer retention fits perfectly with our Purpose," Ashley said.

Everyone nodded.

"I would say that the same applies to our Vision," said Dustin. "And actually, look at our Tenets. We are going to have to do all of those things too. Maximizing our strengths as a team, always keeping our customer in mind, and focusing on quality will impact our Critical Number!"

"I couldn't have said it better myself," Rachel said. "Sounds like your Critical Number is in perfect alignment with your PVTV. You'll want to keep coming back to that and reminding your team of the connection. Your PVTV must work together with The Great Game.

"Let's keep this progress going. Today we're going to talk about the Huddle and Scoreboard. What do you remember about the Huddle from the book?" she asked.

"It sounds like the Huddle is where everything comes together," said Dustin.

Ashley said, "Yeah, I can't wait to have our Huddle meetings!"

"I've always said that the Huddle is my favorite time of the week. But it takes hard work to create a Huddle that focuses everyone on the task at hand."

"How long should our Huddle meeting be?" Megan asked.

"Based on our experience and talking with The Great Game team, 30 minutes is a good amount of time to share all the relevant data and keep everyone's interest," Rachel said.

"How should we structure our Huddle?" Q asked.

"Ultimately, that will be up to you. Here's a basic framework for how to think about it," Rachel said, and she walked back up to the whiteboard.

She wrote:
- ***The Huddle***
- ***The Rules***

- *PVTV*
- *Critical Number*
- *Scoreboard*
- *Areas of Focus*
- *Weekly Game Plan*
- *MiniGame (optional)*

"In our experience, these are the six core areas of the Huddle, in the order of how you'll want to address them. When you have MiniGames running, they would be a critical seventh part of the meeting. Over time, you'll figure out what to adjust, and maybe you'll add a few things. For instance, we recently added a quarterly theme to guide our work and progress measurement," Rachel said.

"Starting with The Rules reminds everyone to stay focused. Our Rules are: Be On Time, Be Present, and Be Curious. We start every meeting by reinforcing these items, so everyone knows how to behave in the meeting," she said.

"And then you go over the PVTV," Megan said. "We've been doing this fun thing in our meetings where one person says the Purpose, and then they call on someone to do the Vision, and it goes like that."

"Love that! After PVTV, you remind everyone of your Critical Number and how you're progressing against it. Then you get into the crux of the meeting—the Scoreboard and your Areas of Focus. The Scoreboard is exactly what it sounds like. It shows how your team is doing from a metrics perspective. And the Areas of Focus are the three to five major drivers of hitting The Critical Number," Rachel said.

"The good news is that you've already done much of the work to identify your Scoreboard metrics and your Areas of Focus," I added.

"Oh, I see! The supporting, trackable data likely are points you're considering for the Scoreboard, and all those areas of opportunity that we listed are potential candidates for our Areas of Focus, right?" Hala asked.

"Bingo," said Rachel. "Every meeting ends with the team coalesced around the priority action items to manage before the next weekly Huddle. But you start by reviewing the previous week's list. Hopefully, each week you'll be able to check off most of the items, and whatever you weren't able to complete would roll over to the current week, assuming they're still applicable."

"How do you put all of this together and keep it running every week?" asked Dustin.

"At our company, we created a deck. We work together to update it every week and project it during Huddle to keep the meeting on track. I would suggest you do that, at least at first. It's a great way to be able to envision how the Huddle will work. You may end up not using a deck, but let's start there," Rachel said.

I could tell that the team was starting to get antsy to begin working on this. Rachel picked up on that as well and said, "So I think this is where we will leave you. Your mission between now and the next meeting is to take a stab at a Huddle deck and Scoreboard. And remember, have fun with it! The Huddle should be engaging and exciting for the entire team."

Megan offered to show us out, but we assured her that we could find our way. As we were about to exit the walled-off area, I turned and took a look at the team.

I said, "Rach, check this out."

She turned and looked back. The team was already broken into two small groups. Each one was at a section of the whiteboard working away. Rachel smiled. It was clear that she was proud to see this team come together around our concept.

"Huh, that looks interesting."

We turned and saw that Shera had walked up behind us. She was looking at Megan's team too.

"Hey, you two," she said. "So what's going on over there? They look pretty animated."

"We've been working on helping them implement a system called, The Great Game of Business," Rachel said.

"Really? Sounds interesting. I'd love to hear more about it." She paused. "Actually, Rachel, if you want to hang out, I have some time. Can you stay and catch up on some upcoming work your team will be doing, and then you can tell me about this Great Game idea?"

Rachel said, "Sure, I'd love to."

We said our good-byes, and I headed out, waving at Rosey on the way.

"Uh, Charles, are you sure this is safe?"

I was looking up at a 50 foot wall. Charles was back in town, and he had somehow talked me into meeting him at the local rock climbing facility on the west side of town.

"Yes, Will. It's fine. And let's get some exercise while we catch up," he said.

I really wanted to catch up with him, so I acquiesced. But not eagerly.

"Oh, come on, Will. It's perfectly safe," he said. He was about eight feet up the wall. "Look, we're all harnessed up, and if you get in trouble, all you have to do is push off."

With that, he let go of the wall and pushed off, and the wire he was connected to slowly lowered him to the ground.

"Ya gotta admit though, the police body sketches on the ground are maybe in poor taste," he said. Indeed, the joke was a bit off-putting.

We started to climb. I quickly found it difficult to talk while trying not to die. Charles, of course, had no problem whatsoever.

"So, you've taken this product team at SalesLive through PVTV and The Great Game?" he asked.

"Yep," I said, hoping he'd keep asking questions that I could answer with one or two words.

"That's fascinating. I'm excited to see it in action. You said I could come to the first official—what do you call the weekly meetings again?"

"Huddles," I said, in between pants.

"Great. I'll look forward to joining you in a few weeks. That's going to be fun to see. It's too bad I'm not building companies any longer. I would have loved to implement something like this," he said.

"It's never . . . too late . . . you know," I said, gasping more than I wished to admit.

At this point, Charles was more than ten feet higher than me on the wall. I could tell he had his sights on the bell at the top, whereas I was too gassed to go any longer.

"I'll see you at the bottom," I said, as loud as I could. Charles gave me a thumbs up and kept climbing. I dug deep for some confidence, let go of the wall, and pushed off. Just like Charles said, the wire lowered me softly to the ground.

Ten minutes later, Charles rang the bell. He pushed off triumphantly and slowly made his way down to me.

"Nice work!" I said.

As he untangled himself from the harnessing, he said, "Thanks! And you did great too. The first time I did it, I could barely make it halfway. Let's get a drink."

We walked over to the cafe area and ordered smoothies.

"So what's left in the process—just one more meeting you said?"

"That's right," I said. "We are going to go through MiniGames and Quick Wins. MiniGames are really fun."

"Fun! Now that's something you don't often hear in business. Indeed, the entire process does sound like fun. I really do wish I had learned of this in the past. I had some teams back in the day that could have benefited from some collaborative fun and team building," he said.

"Really?" I asked. "From what you've told me, I thought your companies always had great cultures."

"I think they did. PVTV helped us keep our eye on the prize when it came to our culture. But I found what you have as you've been on your journey. I found that camaraderie and esprit de corps got lost the larger we grew. It was hard to put my finger on it. I think you're onto something by putting PVTV together with The Great Game," he said.

"Well, I can't wait for us both to see it in action. I have to give Rachel so much of the credit. She implemented the system at our company and ran point on it with the SalesLive team," I said.

"It was a smart move putting her in charge, Will. She was meant to be running the agency, and you were clearly meant to be doing . . . what is it again that you're doing?" he said, laughing.

"Well, it would appear I'm preparing to audition for the next

Mission Impossible movie," I said, looking up at the rock climbing wall we were just on.

Laughing, Charles said, "Speaking of that, ready for round two?"

MINIGAMES & QUICK WINS

One week later, Rachel and I stood in the same spot where Shera had met us, just outside Megan's team area. As we scanned the room, we saw whiteboard after whiteboard filled with writing, charts, and Post-it notes. On the center whiteboard, there was a large chart drawn, with SCOREBOARD written at the top.

"Pretty impressive, isn't it?" Megan said, beaming.

"It sure is!" Rachel said. "Look at all this work your team did!"

"Well, actually, a lot of this is work from the full team. Once we got into the process and wrapped our heads around the key elements of the Huddle and Scoreboard, we started to bring in the other team members. And let me tell you, the team was more engaged in this process than anything else I've ever given them," Megan said.

She gave us a tour around the space so we could see the work. Each whiteboard was dedicated to a different aspect of the Huddle. I could tell by the different handwriting that many people contributed to each whiteboard topic.

After about ten minutes, we made our way to the conference table where Megan's team was waiting. Their smiles made it clear that they were as proud as Megan of their hard work.

"I have to say, it is stunning how much great work you all have done on this," Rachel said. "It wasn't that long ago that we went through this process at our company, and you're bringing back a lot of great memories of how the team came together to work on it."

"This experience felt like the first time you had us start the PVTV process," said Sasha. "I remember that feeling of excitement. Even though I didn't quite understand what we were doing at the start, we were working together as a team on important work for *our* team. I can still feel the energy from that moment. That's what it felt like when I saw the larger team working on this together."

"That sense of belonging, of being in this together, is exactly what we're hoping to unlock," Rachel said.

They spent time talking through their Scoreboard. It had The Critical Number listed at the top and the metrics that would help them achieve it listed below. It read:

	Month 1	*Month 2*	*Month 3*
Customer Retention*			
Net Promoter Score			
Products per Customer			
Delivery Accuracy			

The Critical Number

"We decided to create a template before adding in all the specifics, so you could tell us if we are on the right track," Megan said.

I asked, "Can you walk us through one of the metrics and how it relates to The Critical Number?"

Megan nodded and said, "Q, why don't you take a stab at that."

"Happy to," Q said. "Let's take Products per Customer. In our customer research, we've seen that the number of our products that a customer uses ties directly to how long they stay with us. In the industry, we call this 'sticky.' Basically, it's harder to move to a competitor if they're using multiple offerings from us."

"Plus, if they're using multiple products, that generally indicates that they're happy with us," added Ashley.

"Exactly," said Q. "We believe that if we can increase this number, our customer retention will go up as a result. Right now, the metric sits at 1.7, which means that on average, our customers use 1.7 of our products."

I counted up the supporting metrics they had listed under The Critical Number.

"So you have seven metrics you'll be tracking. How did you get the list down to just those seven? I see from the whiteboards there are quite a lot of factors that didn't make the list."

Hala said, "Once we had the big list from all the team members for us to consider, we used a sorting exercise that Ashley shared with us to get them down to these seven."

"User experience expert, at your service," Ashley said, and we all laughed.

"Well, this is terrific work," Rachel said. "The reality is, you won't know how well you did until you get deep into running The Game. Based on our experience, I'd bet that you'll find that a few of the metrics don't help as much as you thought, and there will likely be a few that you'll want to add. The key will be to listen to your team and watch how they behave."

She stood up and wrote on a blank area of the whiteboard:

Meeting 1: Introducing The Great Game
Meeting 2: The Critical Number
Meeting 3: The Huddle and Scoreboard
Meeting 4: MiniGames and Quick Wins
Meeting 5: The First Huddle

ALWAYS

CONNECT

TO PVTV

"Ready to keep going? I'm excited about today. We get to talk about the fun stuff, MiniGames and Quick Wins! Honestly, I think the whole process is fun, but this is where you'll really get to be creative," she said. "Who wants to take a stab at how we define MiniGames?"

Hala said, "If I remember correctly, MiniGames are basically small incentive plans that target day-to-day improvements, which hopefully add up toward hitting The Critical Number."

"I couldn't have said it better myself," Rachel said. "We've found that MiniGames help boost engagement in The Game and allow us to focus on a particular problem we're facing. Plus, they're a fun way to bring The Great Game to life for everyone."

Rachel reached into her laptop bag and pulled out sheets of paper.

"Lucky for you, I have a handout," she said, smiling. "This is a step-by-step process of how to create an effective MiniGame."

She passed around the sheets, even giving me one. It read:

MiniGame Steps to Success

1. *Select the objective.*

2. *Set the improvement goal.*

3. *Estimate the benefit.*

4. *Identify the players.*

5. *Determine the time frame.*

6. *Create a theme.*

7. *Build a scoreboard, and establish a Huddle rhythm.*

8. *Decide on the rewards, and determine an award schedule.*

9. *Play The Game.*

10. *Celebrate the win.*

The group took a few minutes reading the list, with several making notes on the page as they read.

"I recommend finding something pretty easy for the team to go after at the beginning. Getting some quick wins, with appropriately low but fun rewards, can go a long way to help people get into the process," Rachel said.

"Can we run multiple MiniGames at the same time, or is it better to do them without overlapping?" Dustin asked.

"That's entirely up to you. I might consider starting with a few simple MiniGames that cover the whole team, so everyone has a chance to participate," Rachel said.

"What are some examples of rewards that your agency has used?" asked Sasha.

"Oh, we've tried it all. We've done things like time off, gift cards, lottery tickets, group activities, and tickets to a sporting event. Honestly, for our team, a pizza party is usually the most effective. I think people genuinely enjoy the chance to hang out. You'll find what works best for your team. I encourage you to change it up and keep it fun."

"And we want to have the MiniGames presented somewhere so people can see it at all times, plus review it during the weekly Huddle, correct?" Megan asked.

"Right. Whoever is running a given MiniGame should use the Huddle to get everyone fired up. It's their chance to show off their progress, and it helps with group accountability," Rachel said.

The team had a few more questions, but once again, we could tell the best thing would be for us to get out of their way and let them get to work.

THE FIRST HUDDLE

Rachel and I decided to ride together to SalesLive's office to witness their first weekly Huddle. On the drive over, we were giddy with anticipation.

"I wonder what kind of MiniGames they have cooked up," Rachel said.

"Me too. And I am so interested to see how the full team embraces the concept. You remember our first Huddle at the agency?" I asked.

"You know I do. I'm not sure I've ever been that nervous, actually," she said.

"Well, you and the leadership team did a fantastic job. And overall, the team was pretty into it. Nothing like they are today, of course. Everyone has grown into it."

"For sure. I've read case studies on The Great Game, and it seems like that's pretty typical, that the Huddle takes time to build, but once it does, it should be the most exciting time of the week."

Rachel glanced out of the window. "Hey, that's not Charles, is it?"

I looked out, and sure enough, Charles was in the bicycle lane peddling away.

"It sure is! That crazy guy. I should have known he'd use the commute to SalesLive to get in some exercise," I said.

"Oh, he's coming to the Huddle as well?" Rachel asked.

"Oh yeah, he's really pumped about this latest turnaround. Plus, he's mentored Shera in the past. I don't think I could have kept him away if I wanted to."

We pulled into the SalesLive lot and parked the car. As we walked across the parking lot toward the entrance, Charles rolled up next to us and hopped off his bike.

"Morning, team!" he said.

He locked his bike into the rack by the entrance, pulled off his helmet, and ran a hand through his hair. We all entered the lobby together.

There was no line this time, so we made our way straight to Rosey. She looked up at each of us and said to me, "Welcome back, William."

"Good morning! We're here for the Huddle meeting," I said, reaching out my fist.

She bumped my fist, then looked at Rachel and said, "And you are?"

"I've been coming here for the last month. You don't remember me, but you remember Will?" she asked.

Rosey just looked at Rachel and blinked several times.

After realizing she was not going to win this one, Rachel sighed and said, "My name is Rachel. I'm also here for the Huddle meeting."

"Thank you," Rosey said. She looked over at Charles and said, "Charles, welcome back. Are you also here for the Huddle meeting?"

"Yes, I'm here to observe the Huddle meeting with Will and Rachel. And I'm surprised you remembered me! I think we only met one time, about a year ago, right?"

"That is correct, but I always remember a face," she said.

"Oh, come on!" Rachel huffed. "You're doing this on purpose. Did someone put you up to this or something? I can't believe you'd remember him after . . ."

I grabbed Rachel by the shoulders and started moving her toward the couch, and said to Rosey, "Sorry, don't worry about her. She's liable to *drone* on and on . . ." I emphasized the word drone, hoping Rosey would get the pun.

As we made our way to the couch, we heard Rosey cackling quietly.

A few minutes later, Dustin came to get us. We introduced him to Charles and then followed him through the hallway into the central open area. We could hear the buzz of excited voices emanating from the corner where Megan's team had set up their Huddle area.

Dustin led us through the opening—a makeshift doorway created by two whiteboards pulled together. There had to be well over 50 people in the room, mostly standing. Megan and her team were up front, going over last-minute details.

We grabbed a seat toward the back, and I looked at the time: 9:59 a.m. One more minute until go time.

Just as the clock struck 10:00 a.m., Shera came in and grabbed a seat at our table.

"Hey, you guys! Charles, I didn't know you were going to be here!" she said, hugging him.

"Are you kidding! I just wanted to see if Will finally wrecked your company with one of his crazy ideas," he said, laughing.

Shera smiled and said, "Yeah, me, too. I'm as eager to see what happens today as you are."

Megan asked everyone to take their seats. They did, and after a few seconds, the room grew quiet.

Megan stepped up onto a chair, opened her arms wide, grinned, and shouted, "Welcome to the Product Team Weekly Huddle!"

Everyone cheered, and she said, "Okay, as we do with every meeting, we're starting with our PVTV. Who wants to take the lead?"

A woman at the table next to us raised her hand. Megan said, "Yes, Hanni, the floor is yours."

Hanni stood up and recited the PVTV, stumbling on only a couple of words. When she finished, the room erupted in cheers.

Hala then explained the overview of The Game and how the rest of the Huddle meeting would go. As she talked, a large projector screen began lowering from the ceiling, filling up a large portion of the wall behind her.

When Hala finished explaining the agenda, Megan said, "Okay, let's get into this." Someone flipped the light, and the room got dark. A projection came on screen with the date and "Weekly Huddle."

From that point, Megan and her team took turns with different sections of the Huddle deck. The whole team seemed mostly into it, though they were generally quiet. The leadership team was presenting a great deal of new information for them to digest.

I saw Shera make a few notes on her phone, obviously interested in this experiment. A few times, she leaned over to Rachel to ask a question.

About 20 minutes into the Huddle meeting, Dustin said, "And now it's time for our very first MiniGames!"

He explained that there were going to be three different MiniGames, each running for the next month. With Ashley's help, they explained how each MiniGame would help them toward the goal of hitting their Critical Number.

One of the MiniGames focused on quality assurance. On a big whiteboard, someone had drawn a giant maze. A little magnetic bug was positioned in the far left corner. As the quality assurance team found defects in the software, the bug would progress. There were 35 spots along the maze that the bug could move.

Ashley explained that their goal this month was to have fewer than 35 bugs found. Each time they found one, they'd move the bug forward. As a bonus, the team could move the bug back five spots for every two consecutive bug-free days.

"The best thing is if we finish the month and the bug has not made it to the end, we're going to celebrate by taking everyone to a Crushing Crickets game!"

The Crushing Crickets were the local minor league baseball team—and apparently a crowd favorite. Everyone went nuts when they heard the reward.

The Huddle ended with Megan explaining the weekly game plan. She closed the meeting, and everyone started to cycle out. By and large, everyone seemed excited. I even heard some people talking about ideas they had for reducing the number of product defects.

After everyone cleared out, Megan came over to our table and plopped down.

"Great work up there!" Rachel said. "I know it took a lot of work to get to this point. You must be exhausted."

"I sure am. We were up until 2:00 a.m. last night tweaking the deck, and then we met up at 6:00 a.m. to rehearse and go over any last-minute details," she said.

"Well, it seems to have worked," Shera said. "I'm pretty sure I've just witnessed the future of this company. Let's see how it goes for the next six months or so, but I'd be surprised if we don't adopt this for the company overall."

Charles stood up and said, "Megan, it's great to meet you. I was so impressed with the meeting you just ran. If I can ever be of service, please reach out. Shera has my number."

He said his good-byes and made his way out.

We talked for a few more minutes. Rachel reinforced that it would be important to evolve the Huddle as needed, and I made sure Megan knew how important it was to keep The Game fun.

We could tell that Megan needed to get back to work (or find a corner to sleep in), so we said our good-byes as well.

As we were leaving, I gave Rosey one more fist bump. As I did, she said, shaking her head, "Drone . . . good one, William."

EPILOGUE

I could see Jack Stack's face before I could hear him. He was sitting in what appeared to be his office, and someone on his team was getting him set up for our video conference meeting.

Once his audio connected, he said, "Will, good to see you."

"You as well! Thanks again for doing this. I'm really excited to share the progress we made since our visit with you," I said.

The person helping him said, "You're lucky. Jack prefers face-to-face meetings. The fact that you got him on video conference is quite the achievement."

"Yeah, yeah. Thanks, Bill. I think I have it now," Jack said as Bill left the room.

"So, did your team end up implementing The Great Game?" he asked.

I explained to him that our team had implemented The Great Game and that we had helped Matt's team at Titan to do so as well. Then I shared the process we went through to connect The Game to our PVTV model.

Jack was intrigued.

"You know, that's something that we've talked about with The Game over the years. We knew connecting it to a company's Purpose was important. Would you be willing to talk to some of my team members about how that has worked for you?"

"Of course, any time," I said. "And I think what happened next might actually be more interesting to you."

I walked him through our work with the SalesLive team, explaining how we helped them implement PVTV and The Great Game of Business into a team rather than a company.

"Wow, and how did they do with it?" he asked.

"They've been running it for six months, and their CEO told me last week that she's never seen a team work so well and accomplish so much. In fact, it's gone so well that she's going to implement the system at the company level," I said.

He thought for a moment and said, "The idea of running The Game for teams is also something we have been exploring. Teams have run The Game, of course, but usually, that only happens when the company is also running it. One theory we have is if a team within a large company was succeeding with it, that it might permeate through the entire organization."

"Ah, kind of like a proof point for the rest of the company. I like that," I said.

"Right. Hey, we have our big annual conference later this year.

201

Why don't you come and give a talk to our customers about this new process you've cooked up. I love case studies like this that help to evolve what our customers are doing," he said.

I was thrilled to be invited and committed on the spot, eager to get a chance to share the work we had been doing.

We talked for a few more minutes, and after we said our good-byes, Jack said, "One more thing. I know you've read our books about The Great Game of Business. Maybe you should think about writing a book about the experience of bringing your PVTV together with our Great Game, but specifically for how it could work with teams. If you get that done in time, maybe we could launch it at our conference."

I smiled and told him that was a great idea, even though the truth is I'd already started on the book.

And I had the perfect title in mind: *The Great Team Turnaround*.

YOU MADE IT TO THE END!

I am so truly appreciative that you decided, with millions of books at your disposal, to choose this book to read. And you made it to the end! (Or you skipped ahead, which is also perfectly okay in my opinion.)

By reading this book, you've gone on a bit of a journey with me. While Will is a fictional character, he very much is modeled after me and my life experiences. Some things in this book are almost exactly what I experienced, and some things are entirely made up. In every case, the lessons that he and his team learn are all things that I've experienced and had to overcome during my years as an entrepreneur and leader.

Bringing to life the way in which PVTV and The Great Game of Business can work together to create fast-growing, purpose-driven teams required me to dig deep into what has worked and, perhaps more importantly, what has not worked over the course of my 20-plus years of building businesses. It wasn't until the last few years that I finally hit on this formula for success: create an authentic reason and structure for your team to believe in, and then work hard to make sure your team members actually feel like a team! It's so bloody simple, I'm not sure why exactly it took me so long to figure it out.

That's not exactly true. Upon reflection, I do know why it took me so long to get here.

My business "heroes" when I was a young entrepreneur were of the classic variety. Steve Jobs, Bill Gates, Jeff Bezos, Mark Zuckerberg, and Elon Musk.

And while those leaders have stories of incredible, mind-blowing success, the more you read about their stories and hear from their team members, the more you realize they did so by looking at their team members as resources rather than people. They created brutally competitive and destructive cultures, pushing people to or past their limits in order to beat their competition.

Everything changed when I started learning about a different class of leaders. Each one is a wildly successful and transformative individual who has launched and grown significant organizations. But they've done it with humanity and a higher purpose. This is the list of leaders I now hold up as the real exemplars—Yvon Chouinard, Ben Cohen and Jerry Greenfield, Scott Harrison, and of course, Martin Luther King, Jr. and Bobby Kennedy. These leaders put their heart into what they were doing, and through their passion and focus on making the world a better place, built incredible businesses and movements.

Seeing the difference between these lists of successful people was my first awakening to the idea that you could be successful in the classic sense while also striving to truly make the world a better place. And after much self-discovery, I landed on my personal Purpose of having an out-sized positive impact on the world, and have focused every day since on living into that as best I can.

The second act of this discovery of mine was when I first heard about the book, *The Great Game of Business*. I remember that day so clearly. I was at a lunch with three other business leaders when the book came up. One of the leaders had even been trained in bringing The Great Game to life in their organization. I fired up my Amazon app, ordered the book, and devoured it almost immediately.

Learning about Jack Stack's incredible story, and how he was able to get people to believe that they were all in it together, reminded me of my days playing college tennis. My teammates and I would go to battle together, facing off against other college teams, celebrating our successes and picking each other up when we lost. I loved those guys—still do. Playing with them was the first time I felt like I was part of something bigger than myself, and wanting to do anything I could to help my team be successful.

I had the same feeling with my first company. My college roommate, Raj Choudhury, and I started our web design business, Spunlogic, in the dorm room at UNC-Charlotte. We moved from there to my mother's basement, then to a small office in the back of a fitness center. Our small group of team members worked so hard to make that company successful, deeply believing in each other and the journey we were on.

As the company grew over the years, ultimately reaching 75 employees before we sold the business, that sense of "team" had largely dissolved. Amidst the growth and excitement, my partners and I missed the signs that things were changing from that small group of passionate team members to a business where people had "jobs" and where internal politics were more common than we'd have liked to admit.

After reading Jack's book, I realized that long ago I had given up on the idea of ever having that experience again, much less in a business environment. And then—BAM—I could see it. I could envision taking Jack's model and applying it to my business at Dragon Army. And by then, Dragon Army already had momentum with our PVTV, with our Purpose of "Inspiring Happiness" being the throughline on everything we did.

So we got to work and taught ourselves The Great Game of Business, and once it was in place, I saw the beauty of what the foundation of PVTV and The Great Game could bring to life in an organization.

Once again, I can't thank you enough for spending your time with me, and I wish you great fortune in your business endeavors. And remember to always lead with Purpose.

I hope you're happy,

Jeff

P. S. Feel free to check out my website at jeffhilimire.com. You will find a link to sign up for my weekly newsletter where I tell more stories and insights from my entrepreneurial journey.

ACKNOWLEDGEMENTS

As with all books, they truly are a labor of love. And without the support—and love—from my friends and family, I could never produce these books.

In *The 5-Day Turnaround*, I was very specific with my acknowledgements, and this time I'm going to go the more generic route, with a few exceptions.

Where to begin…

To my Dragons, who continue to indulge me with these book writing escapades. And while we've seen strong evidence that the Turnaround Leadership Series has led to new clients and stronger relationships, I know sometimes the immediate reaction is, "What? Dude, another book?!" That reaction, however, is quickly followed by, "Okay, we know you gotta do it, we got you." Thanks for always having my back! #teamfirst

To my friends, who gave me advice, served as inspiration (even if they didn't know it), and pressure-tested my ideas. You know who you are, and your support was so very appreciated.

To Jack Stack and the team at The Great Game of Business for even entertaining this idea, much less partnering with me to bring it to life. I've admired your business for years and its a dream to find myself in your orbit.

To my growing list of mentors, you'll never know what your belief in me means.

To my family, thank you as always for being such a tremendous source of daily joy and love.

And especially to my wife, Emily. I thank God every day that we found each other.

ABOUT THE AUTHOR

Jeff Hilimire is the best-selling author of the *Turnaround Leadership Series* and an accomplished entrepreneur who has launched multiple organizations and successfully sold two companies. His current business, Dragon Army, is one of the fastest-growing digital experience agencies in the nation. Over the course of 20 years, Jeff has helped guide leaders from some of the most well-known global brands to mobilize growth using a startup mentality.

He is the co-founder and active leader of three nonprofit organizations. 48in48 is a global nonprofit that produces hackathon events, building 48 nonprofit websites in 48 hours. Ripples of Hope advances the growth of organizations focused on business as a force for good in the world. And The A Pledge creates a path for systemic opportunity in Atlanta by inspiring marketing and advertising agencies to commit to matching the diversity of their team to that of our city by 2030.

Jeff lives in Atlanta with his lovely wife, Emily, and their five children. You can follow Jeff's adventures on his personal blog, jeffhilimire.com.

ABOUT THE SERIES

BE THE LEADER YOU ALWAYS WANTED TO BE.

Get to know Will, Rachel, Matt, and their teams as they navigate the opportunities and challenges of a competitive and crowded marketplace. Blending a narrative style and tactical resources, the *Turnaround Leadership Series* is a go-to for leaders seeking to improve how their teams collaborate, endure challenges, and pursue outcomes.

"It's a tactical, inspiring read!"

Ben Chestnut, CEO of Mailchimp

"This is the formula for how every team should run!"

Jack Stack, CEO of SRC Holdings Corporation and best-selling author of "The Great Game of Business" and "Stake in the Outcome"

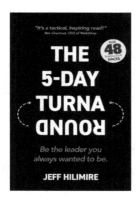  

Create Transformative Growth	Lead Confidently Through Crisis	Putting Purpose Into Practice
For large companies, following well-established processes is deemed necessary for securing the bottom line. But what happens when pursuing the status quo slows progress or, worse yet, creates a setback? The 5-Day Turnaround offers actionable steps for driving growth by thinking and acting like an entrepreneur, even inside mid-sized and enterprise organizations.	Most leaders plan for emergencies. But when a crisis hits, it brings unexpected challenges. In The Crisis Turnaround, Will and his team navigate disruptions to processes, projects, revenues, and teams that come as the result of an unprecedented event. The book is a case study that prepares readers to thrive in crisis and even emerge stronger.	The leadership classic The Great Game of Business (GGOB) has inspired countless organizations to operate with transparency and rigor. The first two books in the Turnaround Leadership Series introduce the Purpose, Vision, Tenets & Values (PVTV) model. In The Great Team Turnaround, these powerful concepts come together to unlock a team's unstoppable potential.

All of the Leadership Turnaround Series books are available on Amazon. If you're interested in booking Jeff Hilimire for a speaking engagement, buying a bulk order for your team, or getting signed copies of any of the books, please contact Jeff directly at jeff@dragonarmy.com.